SEASIDE STYLE

INSPIRATIONAL IDEAS FOR THE HOME

SEASIDE STYLE

INSPIRATIONAL IDEAS FOR THE HOME

ANDREA SPENCER

APPLE

This edition published in the UK in 2007 by
Apple Press
7 Greenland Street
London NW1 0ND
www.apple-press.com

ISBN: 978 1 84543 240 9

This book was designed and produced by
Anness Publishing Ltd
Hermes House
88–89 Blackfriars Road
London SE1 8HA
www.annesspublishing.com

CONTENTS

Introduction

coastline

pebbles

boats

driftwood

wind

shells

waves

beach huts

sand

breakwater

shingle

life belts

The essence of seashore style is the sea itself, stirring powerful, evocative memories of childhood holidays. Every summer our cities empty and we head *en masse* for the coast. To walk across the beach to the water's edge is one of the great joys in life. As our cares and everyday concerns evaporate, we enter a new world of light and space, distance and energy – a world where the elements rule, and wind and waves create an ever-changing environment. Dipping our toes in the ocean, we gaze in wonder at the horizon. Picking up a pebble, we marvel at its shape and pattern and, sensing it to be somehow precious, slip it into a pocket. Squinting into a rock pool, we spy movement and suddenly are children again. By introducing the style of the seashore into our homes, we can bring back these memories and recapture the invigorating sensation of mental and physical well-being that we experience by the sea.

Introduction

As the pace of living increases, so it becomes more essential for people to create a harmonious home environment. Seashore style fulfils such a need – it is a style that can work anywhere, be it a beach hut or a simple cottage, a traditionally understated period room or a fresher approach in modern surroundings.

Seashore style uses materials that improve with the passing of time, and furniture and furnishings that are simple, practical and above all comfortable. Matt, chalky seascape colours feature, as do uneven surfaces and distressed patterns that evoke the ebb and flow of the shoreline. Wood and stone blend harmoniously with each other and with unpretentious canvas, calico and muslin.

Wicker, jute, raffia and rope are combined with seashells and driftwood to give a balanced, homely living space and to provide a restful backdrop for day-to-day existence. Seashore style is calm, easy on the eye, and provides a welcome antidote to life in the fast lane. It is about appreciating the natural environment, taking the time to savour the here-and-now aspect of life.

So, take a stroll along the shoreline and take your inspiration from nature's treasures at the water's edge. Use the colours, textures and natural gifts of the sea as creative themes for beautifying your surroundings. Arrange the mementoes from your seaside strolls simply around your home and let them serve as a reminder of happy, peaceful days spent by the sea.

Left: *Natural materials are at the heart of seashore style. Driftwood and feathers form a striking centrepiece, and shells look attractive arranged in a bowl, sewn on to a table napkin, or attached to the front of a flowerpot.*

Right, clockwise from top left: *A splendid wrought iron verandah, in traditional seashore style; a jaunty weather vane with elaborate curlicues; the weathered colour of life belts; a weather-beaten doorway, painted in familiar seaside colours; old wooden fish-packing crates, with rope handles; a seaman-like knot.*

Seaside Evocations

All seaside homes have an inherent simplicity that imbues the atmosphere with a sense of tranquillity. However, architectural styles do vary around the coastlines of the world, depending on the local climate and resources. The grey stone cottages of the Brittany coast are quite different to the dazzling whitewashed exteriors of the Mediterranean, or the wooden houses of the Baltic and Atlantic.

Nordic Style

As would be expected from a country almost surrounded by water, Scandinavian interiors are intimately bound up with the all-pervasive blues of seas, lakes and sky. In a country

where trees are plentiful and workable stone scarce, it is no surprise to find that the majority of the population lives in wooden or timber-framed houses. In the past, furniture and utensils were made of wood, as were the tools used to build boats and sleds. Planked walls were the preferred building choice and, although painted colours have been used for decoration since Viking times, it was not until the eighteenth century that colour was widely used for cottage interiors, on walls and built-in furniture. Many old cottages still have walls honeycombed with cupboard beds – the one nearest the hearth used to be reserved for the old or ailing members of the family. Winters are cold, harsh and long and

Left: *Found tinware makes an impromptu vase.*

Right: *Bleached floorboards, simple wooden furniture and whitewashed walls: the essence of Nordic style is its simplicity. Here, a beach towel hangs drying over a wood-burning stove.*

Below: *An elegant, old-fashioned shelter on the seafront promenade. You can almost hear the band playing in the distance.*

the summer evenings are sometimes cool, so wood-burning stoves and fireplaces still form an integral part of every home.

Simpler household interiors were painted predominantly in one colour, often a slate blue-green with a few prized pieces of furniture spectacularly decorated. Grey used to be a popular choice, partly because it was considered fashionable and partly because the ingredients were relatively inexpensive. The clear matt colours indigenous to Scandinavia come from distemper and limewash and, being organic paints, they allow the surface to breathe and gently weather over the years. Wooden floors take on a subtly distressed look over the decades as floorboards are bleached by repeated scrubbing with wet silver sand.

Atlantic Style

Battered by the heavy seas and blasted by the icy winds that whistle off the Atlantic, the isolated east coast of America became a haven for rich nineteenth-century Americans who built summer homes there to escape from the stiflingly hot cities and to enjoy the quiet and cool sea air. Wood is the indigenous building material, so these houses were mainly built of clapboard. Although residences initially appeared to be large, much of the space was taken up by the wide surrounding verandahs, providing shade and a pleasant place to sit in the evening cool.

Today, we view light as an absolute must for our continued health and well-being. The sunnier the day the brighter

Above: *A row of beach huts is an essential element in the traditional British seaside. Whether freshly painted or faded and peeling, they always look attractive.*

the room, and the better our frame of mind. Nineteenth-century Americans, in keeping with the dominant fashion at that time, influenced by the Victorians in England, decorated their homes in rather sombre colours, with lots of solid mahogany furniture in every room and heavy curtains draping the windows to keep interiors cool. This was typical of many turn-of-the-century homes, where protection from the sun and heat was deemed more important than ventilation. However, nowadays things have changed. Modern interiors are painted white to enhance the architectural detail and to reflect available light; windows are left free of cumbersome drapes to enjoy the invigorating off-shore breezes. Furniture is kept simple and is left either bare or painted with soft whites or subtle seascape colours. Exterior wood is left in its natural state to reflect light from sunrise to sunset.

English Seaside Style

In many coastal towns in England, houses are gaily painted in fairground colours which soften as they fade in the sun. This creates a pretty patchwork effect, which is accentuated by flowerpots and window boxes, decorative ironwork and old-fashioned verandahs. Piers, esplanades and the old "grand" hotels add to the atmosphere. The north of England has a distinctive seaside style, with buckets and spades, kiss-me-quick hats, donkey rides on the beach and "naughty" postcards. At St Ives in Cornwall, in the south of England, the exceptional quality of the light has inspired countless artists.

Mediterranean Style

The light in Greece is legendary – it has an almost luminous quality which seems to bring out the intensity of colour everywhere. The dazzling sunlight and azure of the crystal-clear water are the basis for many interior schemes where three colours predominate: white, blue and ochre. White, a symbol of purity and cleanliness, is seen in the whitewashed façades that are repainted annually. Blue, the colour of the ocean, from aquas to turquoise through to navy, is used on windows, doors and furniture. Ochre, the colour of earth, terracotta and stone, is an ever-present background.

Once inhabited by modest farmers or fishermen, the tiny island houses, with thick whitewashed stone walls, plank floors and painted wood ceilings, have a simplicity and charm all of their own, and they have become much in demand as holiday homes by those wanting to escape the rat race and opt for the simple life. Overhanging wooden balconies and exterior stone staircases are piled on top of each other in intricate patterns on the densely populated hillsides, and donkey tracks lined with pebbles or whitewashed stones snake through the villages.

Above: *Houses and boats cluster together in this Italian seaside town. Vines provide shelter from the sun on roof terraces.*

Left: *These Greek whitewashed buildings take on a soft pink-and-orange glow in the evening sunlight, against the picturesque backdrop of sea and sky.*

High walls pierced by arches provide areas of vital shade at different times of the day and sun-loving plants sit atop them or in huge terracotta pots in courtyards. Doors are a symbol of Greek hospitality and they are usually made of wood, crowned with decorative flowers, and brightly painted or topped with carved stone. Many such entrances open on to luscious gardens, some of which are decorated with Kroklai, a beautiful mosaic of black and white pebbles traditionally used in the gardens, courtyards and house interiors on the island of Rhodes. There is also a huge range of crafted tables, benches and chairs all used for dining outside.

In summer, doors and windows are kept tightly shuttered against the heat of the day and even fabric and furnishings are kept to a bare minimum to make the most of the cool air generated by thick stone floors and walls.

Italian Mediterranean homes emphasize cool interiors, and geometric-patterned marble floors are popular. Houses are stacked in confusion, interspersed with roof terraces, washing and small gardens. The French Riviera coast, in contrast, is lined with grand villas, hotels and apartments, and luxury yachts are anchored offshore. Houses in the old French ports are still traditional, however, with shuttered windows leading on to balconies full of flowers.

Pacific and Caribbean Style

Pacific style centres on the islands of the South Seas, fanned by balmy north-east trade winds. Ventilation and shelter from the sun are the main priorities, as well as protection from dramatic tropical storms. Houses are often improvised out of bamboo, corrugated iron and whatever comes to hand. Cane awnings shade the sun's rays and giant fans stir the air. Warm, vivid colours look good in the bright sunlight.

Caribbean style also draws heavily on tropical influences. Colours are strong and vibrant, life is lived in the slow lane, fans stir the still air and there is an element of make do and mend as all manner of materials are used within the home – from corrugated iron to tarpaper.

Above right: *Thatched roofs are a feature of Pacific style; here, they blend wonderfully with the prettily painted beach huts.*

Right: *Decorative woodwork on the roof of this West Indian home is reminiscent of waves and the shaping on the verandah brings the sun and its rays to mind.*

Inspirational Elements

True seashore style re-creates the natural beauty of the ocean in your home. It can be as simple as displaying your beachcombing finds on a windowsill, or as complex as drawing on maritime themes to decorate an entire room.

Natural Elements

Take a stroll along the shoreline and you'll find a beachcomber's treasure trove that provides an endless source of inspiration for decorative treatments. Found objects need very little arranging – the simpler the better.

Scoop up a handful of smooth pebbles and look closely at their intricate patterning and veining. Large worn stones look beautiful when casually displayed on shelves, but can also do duty as paperweights, doorstops, hearthside companions, or as a tiny shingled beach around the base of a vase or piece of driftwood. Examine pieces of glass worn almost translucent by the sands of time, and see them transformed into tiny jewels. Place objects along windowsills so they catch the light, fill glass tanks to overflowing with favourite shells or fashion a

Above: *Driftwood can serve equally well as a natural sculpture or as firewood.*

Top and left: *The seashore abounds with wildlife – sturdy plants cling to the cliffs, and sandy crabs scuttle along wooden jetties.*

Above: *Pebbles worn smooth by the ocean have a symmetry and charm that make them perennial favourites as holiday souvenirs and keepsakes.*

Right: *The remains of an old breakwater create strange shapes in the shallows.*

selection to create beautiful mirrors and curtain edgings. Small strands of seaweed may be used to create a charming seascape around the edge of a mirror: the paler variety looks especially stunning when fashioned into a tiny wreath.

Driftwood, worn by the relentless pounding of the sea, becomes a sculpture fit to grace a mantelpiece. Weathered driftwood, with curls of peeling paint still adhering to its contours, can be fashioned into shelves hung from lengths of worn rope. Larger pieces can be crafted into furniture.

Take a closer look at wonderful rusting anchors and weather vanes. Collect shells, driftwood, pebbles and other treasures, and use them as a reminder of the patterns of natural decorating that are the very essence of the seashore.

Seascape Colours

Colour is the easiest and most inexpensive way to transform your home. It can make rooms appear smaller or more spacious and also give an air of vibrancy and vitality. Bring to mind the luminous quality of the sea in the Mediterranean or the Aegean, turning from blue to jade-green as the water hits a sunlit patch of sand, a clear blue English sky with the whiteness of a gull in sharp contrast, or the red and blue hulls of Italian fishing boats as they are tossed around on the waves.

Blue is expansive, like the sea and sky, and it can create calm meditative spaces. Yellow is warming and positive like the sun. Red makes us stop in our tracks and so should be used merely as an accent to inject life. Look at how colours

Above : *The sun gives a roseate glow to the sky and shoreline of this Californian beach as it sets over the ocean.*

Right: *Few views are more relaxing than the sight of moored boats bobbing gently in safe waters, as in this Greek island harbour.*

Left: *The bright primary colours on this life belt and dinghy are pleasing to the eye and would also work well in the colour scheme for a child's bedroom.*

Above left: *Natural materials such as wood and rope weather beautifully. Bleached blues and off-whites are central colours in seashore style.*
Above right: *Alliums grow in abundance on the cliffs; they too are a lovely faded colour.*
Below left and right: *Old fishing nets, floats and life belts can be incorporated in interiors.*

are changed by other colours and by the light in which they are seen. Pale colours create a feeling of light and space while darker tones provide shade and suggest a more sombre mood. Walls painted white keep houses cool, and reflect the sparkling light from the sea and sky.

Develop a colour palette that works best for you by looking at the landscape and seascape and amassing a collection of treasures that please you. Display them on a windowsill or by a fireplace in the room you are thinking of decorating and note how the colours work together – try a selection of glass

worn smooth by the sea in brilliant blues, aquas and greens, the reds and shocking pinks of geraniums set on a cerulean blue cloth, or even chalky white stones and matt white shells juxtaposed with rope and rusty metal.

Charmingly Distressed

Think of the simple seaside huts with weather-beaten timbers, dotted along the coastline where land meets sea. Note how the strong colours have been faded by the elements and use these as a basis for a scheme. Look at fibres and textures found by the

Above left and right: Layers of paint are stripped away by the elements, creating subtle colour effects on wooden surfaces.
Below left and right: The seashore offers strong textural contrasts – fresh white daisies against a piece of
old wood, and thick coils of net.

seashore and see how beautiful they have become with the passage of time: salt-faded fishing nets in soft aquas; life belts worn to a delicate shade of pink; deep blues which have become almost lavender; hulls of boats weathered by the pounding of the sea where successive layers of paint are still visible. Emulate these wonderfully soft colours and flaking paint on chairs and chests of drawers, and distress wood to echo the sun-bleached silver-grey found on exposed buildings and verandahs.

When decorating your home, observe how wooden beach and fishermen's huts differ in their finishes – a beach hut generally has gaily-coloured paintwork, while the wood on a fisherman's hut is left to weather gradually, unadorned. Take inspiration for your decorative ideas from the planking used horizontally or vertically, and look closely at how struts of wood work together to form the ribs of the interiors of boats.

Examine pebbles and shingle which are often inlaid into walls and floors in subtle colours and intricate designs. The most unexpected things, such as small, smooth stones, can be turned into objects of infinite beauty. Copy the intricate knots and splicing of seafarers to fashion your own tie-backs and

chair trims. Note the fine ironwork used on weather vanes, piers, bandstands and shelters and use them as inspiration for shelf brackets, gates or table bases.

Exteriors

As anyone who lives by the coast will tell you, exterior maintenance is a priority and hardwearing paint is the answer. Traditionally, some coastal dwellers used whitewash to withstand the ravages of sea, salt air and storms, although in later years, more resilient, vivid treatments became popular. Armed with a paintbrush and a bright colour, householders embark on the annual ritual of preserving, protecting and promoting their homes. The stark whites of the Mediterranean are in marked contrast to some areas of England and northern Europe where woodwork painted in seaside blues, sunshine yellows and vivid reds stands out wonderfully against the dark grey stone exteriors. Individual expression is all and, while many schemes show a disregard for colour co-ordination, collectively these brave statements create a brash fairground quality that is every bit as much a part of seashore style as their more subtle counterparts.

Cheerful displays of flowering plants are often found by doorways and in seafront gardens. Choose plants that can withstand the strong sea breezes, salty air and sandy soil found near the coast. Prettily patterned weatherboarding, decked verandahs and frontages decorated with simply patterned pebbles add interest, as does the spectacular ironwork found on piers and promenade shelters.

Left: *The seagull's plaintive cry is one of the most evocative of all seaside sounds. This traditional white wooden building has an unusually grand frontage.*

Below: *Weathering adds character to the beams on an old wooden door, set in the whitewashed stone wall of a fishing village. Cheerful flowering plants in pots add a touch of colour.*

62

Top: *A shelter on a promenade serves as a refuge from sea spray.*

Above: *The paintwork on these beach huts mirrors the blue-and-white of the sea and sky.*

Above: *Cobblestones look wonderful on outdoor surfaces, such as patios and garden paths.*

floors

shutters

paving

wall

plaster

Rooms with Sea Views

You do not need to live by the seaside to give your home a seashore feel. Model boats on windowsills, shuttered windows and seafaring pictures all conjure up the ambience of the ocean. Decorate table settings with shells, or paint seaside motifs on to a tabletop. Make the most of a sunny day or starry night and move into the patio or garden and imagine yourself by the water's edge. Put up a beach parasol, or create a shaded area with a canopy made from canvas or sailcloth.

Rooms for Eating

In the kitchen, shelves and cupboards are a must to keep everything ship-shape, so display your china and glass on open shelves or keep it dust-free behind glazed doors. Naive-style shelves can be made from reclaimed timber such as old

Above: *Quarry tiles are a perfect natural contrast in this all-white kitchen. Accessories such as driftwood fish and a model sailing boat give an immediate seaside feel.*

Left: *Display your favourite china, glass and seashore finds on a simple home-made "dresser". Fix tongue-and-groove boarding to the wall before putting up the shelves.*

Right: *A tiny beach hut verandah with an enticing ocean view is an idyllic setting for enjoying a leisurely meal.*

Left: Toy boats look wonderful in windows, with the light shining through the sails. Choose the boat to fit the size of the window.

Below left: The bathroom is the ideal place to display a collection of shells and other seaside finds.

Below right: A simple touch like this navy-and-white striped roller towel gives an instant nautical feel.

floorboards, scaffolding boards or driftwood. Paint them with a colourwash in off-white or chalky blue. Where possible, leave windows unadorned and line windowsills with displays of beautiful old model boats, shells and other seashore finds intermingled with fresh herbs and scented flowers.

Tongue-and-groove boarding is a familiar feature in many seaside homes and it is also an ideal surface for kitchens and dining rooms. Not only does it imbue a room with a certain warmth but it is also architecturally interesting, can hide a multitude of sins and has good insulating properties. Painted a soft white, it looks clean and fresh rather than cold or clinical.

Stone, tiled or wooden floors often prove the most successful combination with all colours and they can easily be mopped and wiped in case of spillages. To soften hard surfaces, use rag rugs or runners in toning colours.

Natural floor coverings would also suit the seashore style and there is a large choice – coir, jute, seagrass and sisal are all hardwearing. They can be fitted or, if you prefer, you can buy individual beach mats bound with coloured cotton tape.

Rooms for Sleeping

Of all the rooms in the house, the bedroom should be the one that is tranquil and relaxing. An all-white room is beautifully romantic and immediately conjures up images of fine voile curtains wafting in the sea breezes, filmy mosquito nets loosely knotted over inviting beds dressed in cool, crisp linens, and shutters keeping out the scorching heat of the midday sun.

An all-white room is not necessarily everybody's idea of heaven, and soft colours look glorious too. Chalky pinks and blues, aquas and delicate greens are all very relaxing choices for a bedroom. So introduce spots of colour in softly distressed seaside shades on chests of drawers, cane furniture and even bed linen. Colour is completely personal and creating the right shade is purely a matter of experimenting, but it is worth remembering that colours change dramatically as the light in the room changes. For instance, a wooden floor in full sunlight can cast a warm glow around an all-white room. To avoid disappointment, first paint colours on to a piece of board or pin a piece of paper to the wall before starting – watch what happens to the colour in different lights throughout the day.

Rooms for Bathing

Bathrooms, although functional, can be leisurely and luxurious rooms – somewhere to unwind and soak away your cares after a hard day. If the space is large enough, install a comfortable chair, have heated rails to warm towels, install good lighting and, above all, make sure that bottles, lotions and potions are within arm's reach of the bath and shower.

Shells are the perfect foil in this watery world; range them along the windowsill so they catch the light, and fill shelves with displays of coral and other mementos of days by the sea. Make fine muslin curtains for cupboard doors and decorate them with tiny mollusc shells. Create a dado using strips of rope with shells and pebbles attached, or introduce a simple line around the wall with clam shells. If you want to go totally overboard, you could cover all the walls with shells, thus turning your bathroom into a delightful underwater grotto.

Above right: This ornate bedhead is made even more charming by the gently peeling paint.

Right: Create a holiday fantasy by suspending a canopy in the shape of a beach hut over seaside-striped bed linen.

Above: *A navy-blue painted dresser makes a stunning background for modern blue-and-white china.*

Left: *A wonderfully cluttered harbour master's office decorated in toning shades of blue.*

Below: *Painted canvas floorcloths are a traditional and practical floor covering. This one shows a knotted rope design.*

Above: *A useful corner for storing oilskins, boots and hats, ready for wet and windy weather.*

Above: *A room with a view needs very little extra decoration – keep the windows simple and uncluttered.*

Rooms for Living

Make the sitting room the most inviting place in the home. It should be a harmonious, comfortable space that is the centre of family life; used for relaxing, playing with the children, entertaining and perhaps even eating.

White is the perfect foil for most colours and creates a neutral and timeless backdrop for furniture and furnishings. Think of white paint washed over brick, tongue-and-groove planking or rough plaster with its straightforward simplicity. Planked wood as a wall or floor surface is both evocative of seaside interiors and visually pleasing. It provides a robust waterproof surface when painted, is interesting to look at and can easily be wiped over with a damp cloth. Salvage yards are often a good source of old wood or floorboards which simply need sanding and sealing or painting.

You can introduce a textural dimension and depth by adopting traditional methods of application such as colourwashing, distressing and ageing. Soft, matt seascape colours provide cool, tranquil backgrounds while bold, luminous colours brushed on to walls with diluted emulsion create an interesting textured finish that is reminiscent of hotter Mediterranean climes.

Whatever background you choose, avid beachcombers and seaside collectors have little difficulty in decorating their home as their many acquisitions add interest to every corner. Not only do natural displays provide a focal point, but they are also a wonderful conversation piece, bringing vitality to a room. Remember, too, that display areas often work more effectively when collections are grouped according to a theme. Balance complementary and contrasting colours and textures, or assemble objects with a common denominator of provenance, shape or material.

Make the most of every available ray of light, and dress windows, if required, to enhance their architectural interest and beauty. Fabrics such as voiles and muslins allow the maximum light to permeate the room and, if window treatments are kept fairly plain, seashells, twists of straw and rope can all be used to give a little extra definition.

Seashore Surfaces

Beach huts are the ultimate seashore dwellings. Identical and simple in shape, the colours of their faded paintwork give each one a distinctive character. Sturdy white bargeboarding outside and tongue-and-groove matchboarding inside create the snug atmosphere of a ship's cabin. Painted white or colourwashed, the interior looks faintly nautical. A combination of sun-bleached fabrics, weather-beaten furniture and touches of maritime colour immediately call to mind the look of a coastal dwelling. By the sea, the elements take their toll on even the most robust surfaces and materials. Strong winds, sunlight and salt spray gradually distress exteriors to create the weathered effects that are typical of seashore style, and so fashionable in interior design. Wood fades to a ghost of its former self, paintwork peels, metal rusts and fabrics fade softly. Enjoy the subtle gradations of tone, texture and colour.

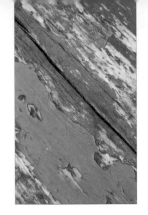

Seashore Surfaces

Walls and floors form the shell of our living space, so it is essential that they create an atmosphere that is both harmonious and comforting. There are many ways of creating a tranquil seashore scheme – the calm neutrality and simplicity of white on white, pale distressed wood, stone and matting are all fine examples. Natural wall treatments have a certain tactile quality that provides an added dimension, from the faintest blush of whitewash over rough plaster to robust matchboard cladding.

Injections of colour can provide instant short-cuts to link a room with nature – from the gentle seashore shades of misty blue, grey-green and sand to the earthy ochres, rich terracottas and the vivid aqua-blues that bring the Greek skies and sea right into your home. Paint suppliers offer a staggeringly large range of colours in different finishes. Even a plain matt colour painted on the wall can provide an ideal backdrop for a seashore theme.

Broken colour and distressed or ageing paint can create informal and interesting walls and woodwork. Part of the charm of natural pigments is their soft, slightly patchy look. Like other natural materials, such finishes age well, fading gently in sunlight. However, care should be taken if using organic paints, such as limewash, which is extremely caustic, or distemper, which is chemically incompatible with modern paint. Apply over fresh plaster or on to a surface that has been completely stripped of previous finishes to prevent flaking.

Above: A simple display of gnarled wooden branches contrasts beautifully with the smooth metal surface of an old galvanized bucket.

Above: Use a small window to frame a still life of shells or coral.

Right: *Distressed surfaces work well together. The pot was washed with paint then decorated with string and glass from the beach.*

Above: *The horizontals and verticals of old fencing and weatherboarding suggest ideas for interior woodwork.*

Left: *Soft blue and white is the perfect seaside colour scheme. The white daisies give a fresh Scandinavian feel.*

Below left: *This fish mosaic makes a colourful, eye-catching focal point for an otherwise rough or uneven floor.*

Below: *The faded colours and texture on this fishing box and tackle are ideal inspiration for distressing walls or furniture.*

Take time when considering how to treat your flooring as it acts as the background for furniture and decoration. Wooden boards are the perfect foil for a seaside look as they are long-lasting and take on a beautiful patina with age. Give them a soft pine look with a coat of matt varnish, or create a chalky white finish by applying either liming paste or a wash of diluted emulsion sealed with matt varnish. Although floorboards are warmer and more yielding underfoot than tiles or stone, weathered stone flags do have a timeless homely quality, and can provide a practical – and hardwearing – solution for areas that connect interior spaces with the outdoors.

Ceramic and mosaic floor and wall tiles now come in a brilliant palette of colours and finishes and give surfaces a luminous and interesting quality. A wonderful idea to evoke the seashore is to embed small fragments of tiles, smooth rounded stones, pebbles or shells into wet concrete to create an original design or border of your choosing.

Above right: Broken shards of blue and turquoise tiles have been set in concrete to make a simple floor surface. Choose harmonious colours, break the tiles into tiny pieces and set in wet concrete. Old china plates can also be used.

Right: Deck chairs and beach huts on an English beach – simple structures of wood and canvas, perfectly at home in the context of beach, shore and sky. The strong blues, greens and reds fade gently in the sun and spray from the sea but still provide an attractive contrast with white façades.

Mediterranean hues: *colourwashed walls*

Use this carefree colourwashing technique to create a wall with a difference. It's ideal for covering large, uneven surfaces quickly and easily, and by choosing colours reminiscent of the sea, an authentic ocean mood can be evoked in no time. Not only can you experiment with colour, but you can also try different textures – apply the paint with a sponge, cloth, wallpaper brush, bunch of long feathers or a wide household brush and you'll get a pleasingly different result each time. Pale colours work best on a white or off-white base to give the feeling of a casually applied wash. However, you can achieve a stronger look and more Mediterranean effect, as here, by using a dark shade for your base with an even darker tone over the top.

YOU WILL NEED:
- **Emulsion paint, in two shades of blue, one slightly darker than the other**
- **Paintbrush**
- **Paint pot**
- **Natural sponge**
- **Soft cloth (optional)**

1 Apply two coats of the lighter blue to cover the surface totally. Leave to dry thoroughly.

2 Dilute the darker shade of paint in the proportion 1:1 with water and apply it with a sponge in a circular motion.

3 Rub over the edges with a soft cloth or sponge to avoid joins.

4 Finally, dab paint in areas which are too light or show marks.

Bright whites: *plaster wall*

If you are lucky enough to have smooth walls but you want something with a little more interest and depth, you can create a slightly rough plaster wall with this technique. The added dimension pleasantly alters an otherwise plain surface and it is easily achieved with a little plaster filler scraped over the surface. For a much more subtle finish, the plaster filler can simply be added to the paint and brushed over the wall surface to give a very light texture. Here, a crisp white painted finish evokes whitewashed cottages by the seaside, but the wall could just as well be washed over with any colour of your choosing. Experiment with turquoise and splashes of vermillion in furniture, soft furnishings and even flowers, and revel in images of the sun-baked Mediterranean.

YOU WILL NEED:
- **Plaster filler**
- **Bucket**
- **Stirrer**
- **Piece of thick card**
- **or plywood**
- **White emulsion paint**
- **Paint pot (optional)**
- **Paintbrush**

1 Following the manufacturer's instructions, mix the plaster filler in a bucket.

2 Wipe it on to the wall with a piece of thick card or plywood so that it forms an uneven surface. Leave to dry.

3 Alternatively, for a slightly smoother result, mix plaster filler and emulsion paint together and brush on.

4 When dry, apply a second coat of emulsion paint, rubbing it in well with the paintbrush so that all the raised surfaces are thoroughly covered.

Sunbleached: *crackle glaze shutters*

Crackle glaze is an excellent medium for ageing new doors, shutters or even furniture. It is easy to apply, and when sealed with a matt varnish it provides a permanent finish with an air of dignified age. The crackle glaze itself should always be applied between two layers of water-based emulsion. This sandwich of paint–glaze–paint allows the surface of the glaze to crack and split, creating a peeled patina reminiscent of ageing paint. Once all three layers have been applied, the shutter should then be sealed with a natural varnish such as shellac.

YOU WILL NEED:
- **Cloths**
- **Sandpaper**
- **Emulsion paint, in aqua-green and blue**
- **Paintbrush**
- **Crackle glaze**
- **Paint pot**

1 *Dust and clean the wooden shutter to prepare it for treatment.*

2 *Rub down the surface of the shutter with sandpaper to provide a key, then buff it up with a soft cloth.*

3 *Apply two coats of aqua-green paint to the shutter, leaving it to dry thoroughly between coats.*

4 *Apply a thin coat of crackle glaze all over the surface of the shutter and leave it to dry thoroughly.*

5 *Water down some blue paint in the proportion 2:1, water to paint, and apply it to the surface. Leave to dry and crack.*

6 *Gently sand over the blue paint to distress and to allow the crackleglaze and aqua-green paint to show through.*

Aqua cladding: *tongue-and-groove wall*

Tongue-and-groove boarding is the perfect solution to create an instant seashore feeling within your home. It's warm to the touch, architecturally interesting and can conceal walls which are in poor condition. However, do not use this technique on walls that are damp. Boarding or planking can be used throughout the home and, once painted, it provides a waterproof surface ideal even for the bathroom. If you don't want to cover walls, then use it on the ceiling where it looks just as attractive. After fixing, either leave the boards natural, varnish them or paint them in a matt colour. Make sure you buy enough boarding to complete the work – if you have to use a few boards from another batch, the machine used to shape the tongues and grooves may not be set to exactly the same tolerance, and the joints might not fit.

YOU WILL NEED:
- **Tape measure**
- **Marker pen**
- **Drill**
- **Hammer**
- **Wall plugs**
- **Spirit level**
- **5 x 2.5 cm (2 x 1 in)**

planed or sawn softwood battens
- **Screwdriver**
- **5 cm (2 in) screws**
- **Tongue-and-groove boards**
- **Tenon saw**
- **2.5 cm (1 in) panel pins**

- **Nail punch**
- **Sandpaper**
- **Emulsion paint, in two shades of aqua**
- **Paint pot**
- **Paintbrush**
- **Cloth**

1 Measure and mark positions 40 cm (16 in) apart down the wall for the battens. Drill holes in the wall on the marked positions.

2 Hammer wall plugs into the drilled holes.

3 Using a spirit level, align each batten to produce a vertical flat plane across the wall.

4 Mark the positions for the screws on the battens and drill the holes. ➤

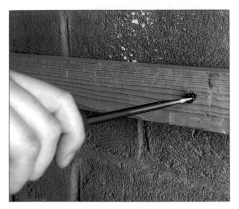

5 *Fix the battens firmly to the wall with the screws.*

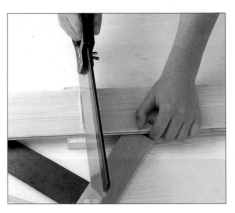

6 *Mark out the tongue-and-groove boards with the pen and cut them to length using a tenon saw.*

7 *With the grooved edge against the left-hand wall, plumb the first board with a spirit level.*

8 *Nail the board to the battens through the centre of the face using panel pins. Use 4 cm (1½ in) pins when fixing boards directly to a timber-framed wall.*

9 *Slide the next board on to the tongue, protecting the edge while you tap it in place with a hammer. Fix the board to the battens: drive a pin through the inner corner of the tongue at an angle. Sink the head below the surface with a nail punch. Slide on the next board to hide the wooden fixing and repeat to cover the entire wall. Sand the holes till even.*

10 *Dilute a pale aqua emulsion paint in the proportion 1:1 with water and brush it on to cover the surface evenly.*

11 *Wipe off any excess paint with a dry cloth. Leave to dry thoroughly.*

12 *Apply a darker shade of aqua by brushing it on in random strokes.*

13 *Wipe off any excess paint with a soft cloth and leave to dry thoroughly.*

Washed out: *decking and floorboards*

Floorboards are the perfect starting point for a seaside interior as they bring to mind ships' decking and beach huts. Liming the boards creates a soft, weathered look that is reminiscent of a Scandinavian interior. This effect can also be achieved by simply bleaching the boards and scrubbing them vigorously every time you clean them – this leaves the boards looking fresh, but you must be prepared to scrub them on a regular basis to avoid any staining and darkening. A quick and effective way to whiten boards is to apply a coat of diluted emulsion, or a mixture of white pigment and linseed oil. Alternatively, you could sand then wax or seal the boards (in their natural state) with several coats of matt or gloss transparent sealer. There are of course many other ways of decorating floors, such as with checkerboard designs and smart shell-motif borders, so here are a few examples to get you thinking about revitalizing your floors.

Limed Boards

YOU WILL NEED:
- **Wire brush**
- **Liming paste**
- **Fine steel wool**
- **Fine, clear paste wax**
- **Soft cloths**

1 Stroke the floorboards with a wire brush, working gently in the direction of the grain.

2 Apply the liming paste with some fine steel wool, making sure that you fill in the grain as you work.

3 Working on a small area at a time, rub the liming paste into the boards in a circular motion. Leave to dry thoroughly.

4 Remove the excess by rubbing in some clear paste wax with a soft cloth. Buff the surface with a soft cloth to give a dull sheen. ➤

"Bleached" Boards

(see opposite page)

YOU WILL NEED:

- **Small tube of white zinc pigment or tint**
- **Raw linseed oil**
- **Mixing bowl**
- **Spoon, for mixing paint**
- **Cloth**
- **Matt varnish**
- **Wide paintbrush**

1 Mix the tube of zinc into the linseed oil. About 2.5 litres (3¼ pints) of the mixture covers 25 sq m (25 sq yd).

2 Apply the zinc mixture to the floorboards with a cloth, rubbing against the grain to begin with.

3 Then work the mixture into the floorboards, rubbing along the grain. Leave to dry thoroughly.

4 Seal with a matt natural varnish, or just apply another layer of white zinc when the first treatment wears away.

Whitewashed Boards

YOU WILL NEED:

- **White emulsion paint**
- **Mixing bowl**
- **Measuring jug**
- **Spoon, for mixing paint**
- **Wide paintbrush**
- **Sandpaper**

1 Dilute the white emulsion paint with cold water.

2 Using a wide paintbrush, brush the whitewash over the floorboards lightly and evenly. Leave to dry thoroughly.

3 Finally, rub the surface of the painted floorboards gently with sandpaper to give an aged effect.

Pebble-dashed: *stone and pebble paving*

Pebbles, cobbles and stone have all been used the world over to create beautifully classic yet hardwearing floors. Many floors, such as those found on the Greek islands, are fashioned into incredible mosaic designs. Others, sometimes seen in old houses owned by ships' captains, depict nautical subjects such as an anchor or a ship and compass. The simple checkerboard design here looks stunning in its simplicity and is not in fact at all difficult to create. So, forget about the more traditional paving ideas available, and have a go at bringing this real feel of the seaside to your feet as you walk about your home.

YOU WILL NEED:
- **Sharp sand**
- **Cement**
- **Straight edge**
- **Tiles**
- **Hammer**
- **Pebbles**
- **Soft brush**
- **Watering can, with a fine spray nozzle**

1 Mix equal quantities of sharp sand and cement. Pour this dry mortar on to the flat surface to be paved. Using a straight edge, level it out until it is smooth. Remove a small quantity so that the mixture does not overflow as you work.

2 Position the tiles, creating alternate squares in a checkerboard effect, making sure they are absolutely square. Hammer them firmly into position and check that once the pebbles are inserted the floor will be level.

3 Arrange your pebbles in a pleasing design, then press them firmly into place. If necessary, hammer them in.

4 Brush dry mortar evenly over the finished surface. Using a watering can, dampen the surface. As the mortar absorbs the moisture, it will set hard.

Seascape Fabrics

curtains

bed linen

cushions

table linen

embroidered

dyed

painted

muslins

blinds

ginghams

flags

striped

The sound of fabric caught by the wind recalls being on a sailing boat at sea or listening to windsocks in a yacht marina on shore. In summer, leave windows open to the sun and sky, and allow unlined curtains to blow free. Lightweight cottons, voile and muslin will lift gently with the slightest breeze and your spirits will lift with them. Seashore fabrics are best kept simple – natural linens, cottons and canvas, with blue-and-white stripes, or ginghams and checks to give bold accents of pattern. Spacious interiors with predominantly white surfaces can be transformed by judicious spots of colour – faded fabrics in washed-out greens, blues and pinks create an atmospheric quality that brings to mind respectively the sea, sky and sun. Modern fabrics incorporating natural fibres such as hemp and raffia fit in well with the seaside theme. For an instant nautical look, fly the flag in royal blue, navy, white and red.

cushions

bed linen

curtains

embroidered

table linen

Seascape Fabrics

Natural fabrics such as cotton, canvas, linen and muslin offer a wide range of textures, weights and finishes to act as a basis for creative work. From the coolness of linen to the translucence of muslin and the firmness of heavier-weight canvas, many different techniques can be used. Fabrics can be fashioned into simple swathed curtains with delicate shell edgings, or constructed into a nautical striped canvas hanging that resembles a ship's awning. Remember that it is often the simpler colours and fabrics that work best.

White linen is timelessly elegant, cool and refreshing and it is beautiful when draped on beds or tables. The popularity of linen has risen enormously over the past few years and, although it is quite expensive, it is a hardwearing fabric which makes it a perfect choice for curtains, sofa covers and cushions. Pure cotton is the most versatile of all furnishing materials – it is soft, strong, hardwearing and fairly inexpensive, so calico and voile can be used in large quantities. Muslin has been used for centuries as a way of diffusing light, and a swathe draped over a pole must be the simplest and easiest of all window treatments. Muslin can simply be tied, looped, clipped or laced on to a pole or rod to make a striking feature of the way it is hung.

Stiffer cottons that block the light, such as cotton duck, canvas or ticking, are equally affordable and hang well. However, they look most attractive when rigged up like sails, lashing the material on to a pole or rod with a rope threaded through eyelets. Chandlers and yachting stores supply a huge range of ropes, pulleys and cleats that can be pressed into service to create an authentic nautical look. Thinking laterally, you can also use other items such as lengths of driftwood or bamboo as poles.

Cushions, chair covers and throws are not essential, but provide an instant way of adding warmth and comfort to a

Left: *Make simple curtains for a bathroom cabinet or window by stitching knots of raffia and string and small shells on to white voile.*

Right: *Mosquito nets give an instant image of romantic tropical shores. Stitch a few delicate starfish and seahorses to the net.*

Left: *A prettily checked duvet cover is left out to air in the warm summer sun and sea breeze on a verandah of a beach house. Soft blue and white cottons are the essence of seashore style. Large checks and ginghams mix well with smaller ones, and with stripes.*

room. They are relatively inexpensive to make and are a good starting point for a less experienced dressmaker to work with. Choose your fabrics to correspond with the seasons. In summer, work with whites, aquas and blues which are reminiscent of seas and skies in tropical climes. In winter, make colours warmer and more comforting with cosy navy-blue blankets and co-ordinating cushions, or muted blues and greens for soft furnishings. Light fires and lanterns to cast a glorious warm glow over the scene and don thick fishermen's sweaters and woolly ribbed socks for complete seashore ambience.

One of the simplest ways to add a nautical look to a room is by using cotton flags. Make them up into cushion covers or

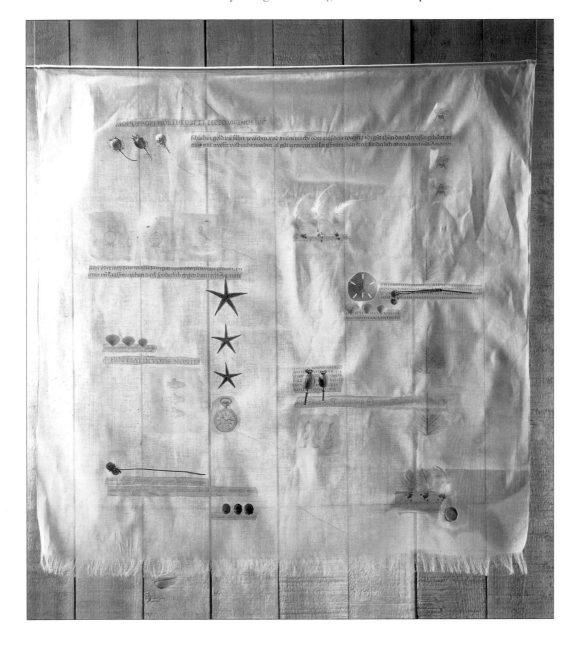

Above: *Dress up simple muslin curtains with a pretty shell edging. Thread the shells first on a length of wire so they are easy to remove when the curtains are washed.*

Left: *This ethereal screen is made of stiffened muslin embellished with a combination of shells, starfish, feathers and dried seedheads. The tongue-and-groove wall in the background reinforces the maritime theme.*

join several flags into a giant patchwork bedspread, backed with blue or red cotton lining. Add a layer of wadding in the middle for warmth on chilly nights, if you wish. You can also make your own simple flags. Felt is the ideal fabric for these, as it is easy to work with and never frays. Use multicoloured flags to decorate the top of a blind or a cupboard – or as jaunty bunting around a child's room.

Heavy deck-chair canvas comes in many delightful colours so use it not only for deck chairs but also to cover cushions and director's chairs, or to make blinds. If the fabric piece is not wide enough for your window then simply attach eyelets down the sides of two separate panels. Lace both panels together to form a larger fabric piece which is not only a more suitable width to function as a blind, but also has a visually interesting central section.

Left: *Multicoloured flags provide startling splashes of colour against a clear blue sky and inspiration for interiors; for example, to brighten up a child's room.*

Above: *Blue-and-white fabrics look wonderful bleached by strong sunlight. The effect is very Scandinavian.*

Left: *A royal-blue and white striped towel spells instant summer seaside, even in the most suburban bathroom.*

Right: *Give cushions a bold nautical look by inserting brass rivets at regular intervals around the edges and threading them with white cord or rope. Make the holes in minutes with a hole punch.*

Shoreline dining: *shell and driftwood tablecloth*

Transform a crisp linen cloth into a three-dimensional work of art by adorning it with tiny bundles of driftwood and delicately coloured shells. This tablecloth creates a beautiful setting for an outdoor dinner party on a summer's evening, and is bound to remind all guests of happy times by the sea. All the adornments are wired on so they can be removed easily when the cloth needs washing. As a stunning centrepiece for your table, mussel shells filled with wax and used as candles are hard to beat. Or, fill a large glass dish with water, place white shells and stones at the bottom and float candles or flowers on the top for a romantic setting. As a *pièce de résistance*, make an ice bowl with tiny shells set within the ice and fill with shrimps, prawns or even oysters for a real seafood treat.

YOU WILL NEED:	
• Pieces of driftwood	• Scissors
• Craft knife	• Glue gun and sticks
• Jute string	• Shells
• Jeweller's wire	• Drill (optional)

1 Cut the driftwood to length with a craft knife, about 4–5 cm (1½–2 in).

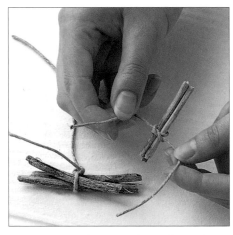

2 Tie the lengths in small bundles with jute string and knot tightly to hold them firm.

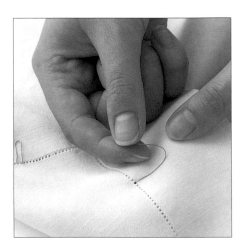

3 Take the jeweller's wire and cut it into 6 cm (2½ in) lengths.

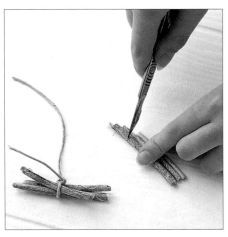

4 Using a glue gun, place a spot of glue on to a shell and press the jeweller's wire firmly into position until the glue sets and the wire has bonded firmly with the shell.

5 If the shells are pre-drilled, or you have drilled them yourself, a piece of string can be threaded through and knotted in the same way as the driftwood bundles.

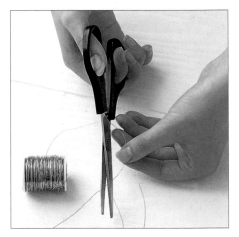

6 To attach the bundles and shells with string to the cloth, thread a piece of wire under the string and secure it firmly. Thread the wire through the piquéd edge and wind into a "U" shape to hold it firm.

Seafarers' luggage: *duffel bag*

A perennial favourite, the duffel or kit bag is reminiscent of seafaring folk leaving the safety of the land for their travels and adventures on the water. Here, a hardwearing white cotton drill is decorated with small strips of driftwood gathered from along the shore. Canvas makes a good alternative fabric. Choose a colour that suits your taste – a deep navy, vibrant red or the vivid turquoise and aqua-blues of hotter climes would all work just as well as a brilliant white or soft cream. All age groups love this kind of bag, and you'll soon find that everybody is keen to fill it with

their personal treasures as they head for the beach during the long days of the summer months.

YOU WILL NEED:
- **Plate**
- **Cotton drill or canvas**
- **Pencil or tailor's chalk**
- **Scissors**
- **Tape measure**
- **Dressmaker's pins**
- **Needle and matching thread**
- **Eyelet pack**
- **Hammer**
- **Masking or yachting tape**
- **Cord**
- **Piece of driftwood**

1 *Decide what size you want your bag to be. To make the base, draw around a plate on to your fabric, using a pale pencil or tailor's chalk. Cut out the shape, allowing 1.5 cm (⅝ in) for the seam.*

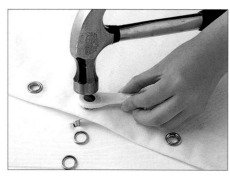

2 *Measure out the side of the bag to give the depth you want, again allowing for seams and a top turnover, and cut it out. Turn over the top of the bag, pin it down and hem along it. Mark evenly spaced positions for the eyelets. Fix the eyelets along the top hem.*

3 *Next, make a small cotton or canvas tag on the base of the bag to hold the drawstring cord.*

4 *Pin, tack and sew the base of the duffel bag to the side.*

5 *Fasten masking or yachting tape to the end of the cord to prevent it fraying. Fold the cord in half and loop through the tag. Thread the two ends through the loop and pull it up in a hitch knot to secure firmly to the tag. Fix the driftwood piece in the knot.*

6 *Knot the pieces of rope at the top of the bag before threading them through the eyelets. Thread the rope through all the eyelets to complete the drawstring.*

Seaside stripes: *beach hut curtain and cushions*

This is a wonderfully simple hanging which can be adapted to suit any room or decorative style. Here, a striped canvas is hung from a bamboo pole to hide deck chairs and other beach paraphernalia from view. Alternatives include using calico for a sitting room, muslin for a bedroom, ginghams for a kitchen and a cheerful striped deck-chair fabric for a child's room. In order to see the hanging clearly, fullness of fabric is not required so the project is extremely economical to make. Smart buttoned cushions scattered casually through the room co-ordinate with the canvas hanging to complete the fresh beach hut style.

Curtain

You will need:
- Tape measure
- Canvas
- Scissors
- Dressmaker's pins
- Needle and tacking thread
- Matching sewing thread
- Dressmaker's pencil
- Eyelet pack
- Hammer

1 Measure the width and drop of your window or area you wish to curtain off and cut the fabric to size. Turn under a 5 cm (2 in) hem on the top and bottom. Pin, tack and sew using two lines of stitching.

2 Measure 2.5 cm (1 in) in from either edge at the top of the curtain and mark the position for the first eyelets. Divide the remaining width of fabric into regular intervals for the eyelets allowing about 13 cm (5 in) space between each one. Mark the positions. ➤

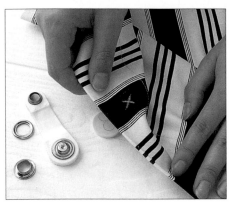

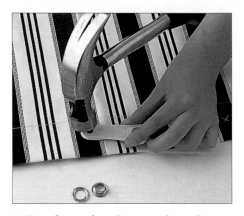

4 Attach the eyelets, following the manufacturer's instructions.

5 On a flat surface, hammer the eyelets firmly in place.

Striped Cushions

(see opposite page, front)

<small>YOU WILL NEED:</small>

- **Tape measure**
- **Cushion pads**
- **Fabric**
- **Scissors**
- **Needle and matching thread**
- **Velcro tabs**
- **Buttons**

1 Cut a length of fabric two-and-a-half times the length of the cushion, plus a seam allowance. Fold over the fabric for twice the length of the cushion pad, leaving the extra half-length for the flap. Sew the seams.

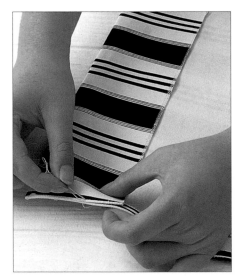

2 Seam down both edges of the flap and trim the corners. Attach Velcro tabs along the length.

3 Sew buttons along the outside of the cushion flap. Insert the cushion pad then turn the flap over and fasten with Velcro.

Button Cushions

(see right, back)

YOU WILL NEED:

- Tape measure
- Cushion pads
- Fabric
- Scissors
- Needle and matching thread
- 1 m (1 yd) cotton tape,
  1.5 cm (⅝ in) wide
- Buttons

1 Measure the cushion pad and cut the fabric to size. You need twice the length plus seams of 2.5 cm (1 in) and once the width plus side seams of 1.5 cm (⅝ in).

2 Turn under a hem at each end of the fabric and seam along on the right side. Pin the tape in place.

3 Tack and sew the tape in position on the right side.

4 With wrong sides together, fold the fabric in half and join the side seams.

5 Mark positions for the buttons and sew them in place.

Ocean blue: *dyed linens*

Using dyes must be one of the quickest, easiest and most fun ways of transforming a piece of fabric. Dyes can refresh tired whites and pale colours and revitalize jaded and worn clothes and linens. Instead of casting out your old favourites, just apply a bit of imagination and some fabric dye and before you know it you will have created a whole new look. Here, a piece of muslin is tie-dyed to give it the pretty aqua colour of the ocean stretching into the distance.

Co-ordinating cushions are dyed to match. If you want to create a darker ocean feel in your home, choose a dark blue dye and imitate the ambience of a more dramatic shoreline.

YOU WILL NEED:
- **Muslin**
- **Needle and matching thread**
- **String**
- **Fabric dye**
- **Glass bead or marble (optional)**

1 Turn under a double hem and slip stitch around the muslin to neaten the edges.

2 On a flat surface, fold the hemmed muslin fabric in half, then fold it in half again.

3 Taking the centre point of the folding, squeeze the muslin together tightly and bind around it with string so that when the fabric is dyed these areas (which will form circles) will be paler. Dye the fabric following the manufacturer's instructions.

4 To make smaller circles, tie a glass bead or marble into the corners and bind around tightly before dyeing.

Seashore dreams: *embroidered pillowcases*

Fall asleep to the sound of the seashore with pillowcases that are guaranteed to evoke blue skies, drifts of clouds, and waves with tiny foaming edges. The co-ordinating blue-and-white scheme is gloriously fresh; a chain stitch and a single strand of thread creates a deliciously delicate feel to the embroidery of the sea creatures and shells adorning the pillowcases. Use a shade of deep sky-blue on the crispest of white linens and set off the blue of the other pillowcase with snowy white stitching. Look out for pictures of shells, fish, mermaids or even lighthouses to decorate your pillows and experiment with different sizes to see whether you prefer a single image in one corner, a border around the edge of the pillowcase, or perhaps one image in the centre of the pillowcase.

YOU WILL NEED:

- **Pencil**
- **Thin card**
- **Tracing paper**
- **Pillowcase**
- **Scissors**
- **Dressmaker's pins**
- **Dressmaker's carbon paper**
- **Dressmaker's pencil**
- **Needle and embroidery thread**
- **Ruler**
- **Cord (optional)**

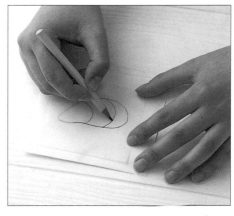

1 Copy the templates from the back of the book on to card, or trace your own design.

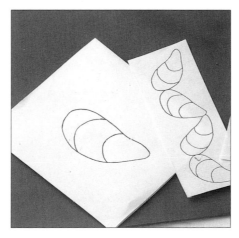

2 Scale the images up or down to suit the size of your pillowcase design.

3 Copy the images on to tracing paper and cut them out. Arrange them around the edge of the pillowcase until the desired effect is achieved. ➤

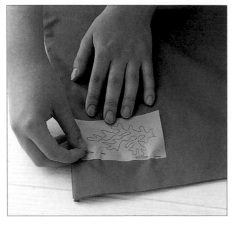

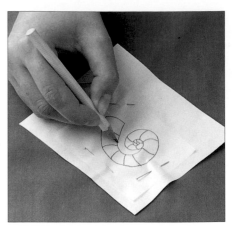

4 *Pin the pieces of tracing paper in place once you are happy with the design.*

5 *Next, pin sheets of dressmaker's carbon paper under the tracing paper in the marked positions.*

6 *Trace over the images with a dressmaker's pencil to leave a clear outline on the fabric.*

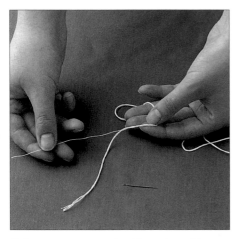

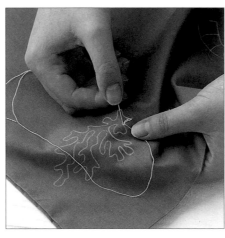

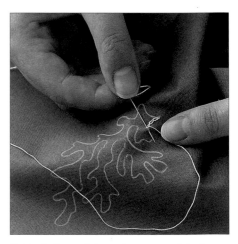

7 *Separate your embroidery thread into single strands to work the chain stitch.*

8 *Start the chain stitch by making a loop and pushing the needle into the fabric on the line of the image.*

9 *Push through into the centre of the loop, following the line of the image.*

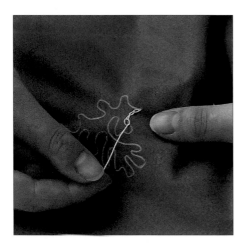

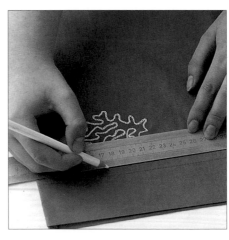

10 *Pull the thread taut. Always try to keep stitch lengths and tautness of thread even throughout the embroidery.*

11 *Mark an edging with a ruler for the top of the pillowcase.*

12 *Finish the edge of the pillowcase with a simple line of cord, or with a double row of chain stitch.*

Blue and white: *squab cushion*

This novel idea transforms everyday tea towels into a wonderfully comfortable padded seat. The crisp white and blue colours are evocative of the seaside, and they give a truly fresh feel to these generous cushions. This technique is used on mattresses in many countries, such as Greece, where they are often filled with cotton or natural horsehair. However, a cheaper and just as effective alternative is wadding or cotton bump. Once you've made your cushion, experiment with it: use it indoors or out, or why not make a few cushions and stack them on a window recess to make an inviting seat?

YOU WILL NEED:
- **2 cotton tea towels**
- **Scissors**
- **Dressmaker's pins**
- **Needle and tacking thread**
- **Wadding**
- **Matching cotton thread**
- **15 cm (6 in) pieces of embroidery thread**
- **Quilting needle**

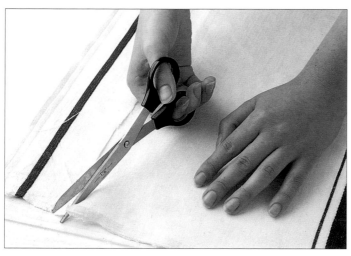

1 Cut one tea towel down to form the base of the cushion cover. The other tea towel forms the top and sides.

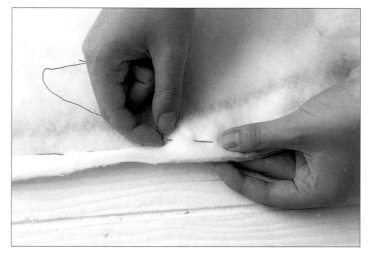

2 Pin and tack a thin layer of wadding to the wrong side of both tea towels.

3 Put the tea towels right sides together and join the top section to the bottom section. Leave a gap open at one end so it can be filled with wadding.

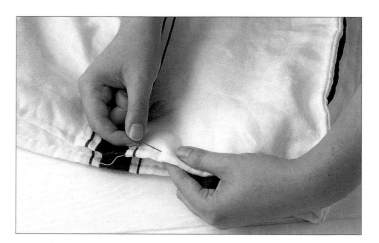

4 On the right-hand side, make a seam allowance of 1.5 cm (⅝ in) by pinching 2.5 cm (1 in) of fabric into a raised section. Pin, tack, fill the cushion with wadding and sew with a running stitch. ➤

5 *Fill with wadding and stitch the opening closed.*

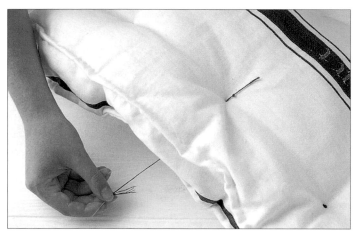

6 *Mark the positions of the quilting points on the top and bottom of the cushion. Double knot the embroidery thread at the end and thread it on to a thick quilting needle. At each of the marked quilting points, thread right through the cushion.*

7 *Double back the thread through the cushion and knot again. Fix decorative knots on the top with a small stitch.*

Watery motifs: *shower curtain*

Give your shower room a feel of the great outdoors with this refreshing scene of starfish, shells and seaweed swaying gently, as though rocked by an ocean current. The clear shower curtain provides a watery backdrop for you to create your very own seaside mood with whatever marine motifs you choose. The example shown here uses a monochromatic, crisp scheme, but you could equally well work with warm, bright, vivid colours to give the project a lively Mediterranean feel.

YOU WILL NEED:
- **Pencil**
- **Paper**
- **Clear plastic shower curtain**
- **Scissors**
- **Masking tape**
- **White waterproof paint**
- **Paintbrush**

1 Copy the templates from the back of the book, or alternatively trace your own design on to paper.

2 Reduce or enlarge the images to fit your chosen design for the shower curtain.

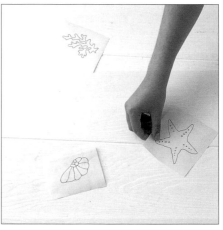

3 Cut out the paper templates or designs and arrange them on the shower curtain as desired.

4 Position the paper templates on a large tabletop in the desired pattern and secure them in place with masking tape. Use a table with a tough surface that won't be harmed by the masking tape.

5 Place the shower curtain over the top of the images and tape it down firmly. Using white waterproof paint, carefully paint the images on to the shower curtain surface. Leave to dry thoroughly before hanging up.

Seaside Furniture

shelves

chairs

tables

mosaics

rope

timber

storage

bedheads

string

wicker

pallets

planks

Beachcombing is the inspiration and the theme when you decide to furnish a room in seashore style. Steamer trunks and wicker laundry hampers have an evocative seafaring charm and serve as flexible holdalls for bedding, blankets or toys. Planks of reclaimed timber and driftwood make rugged chairs and cupboards, full of character. Hunt through junk shops and salvage yards for old furniture, floorboards, wooden crates and pallets, all of which can be stripped and varnished or painted. Alternatively, you can imitate the beautiful silvers and whites of aged, weatherworn wood by distressing modern furniture. Transform a damaged or dull tabletop with a painted shell design, or collect real shells and use them to create a richly encrusted surface. Authentic seashore-style chairs are those specifically designed for lazy days in the sun – wicker chairs, director's chairs and, of course, traditional deck chairs with striped canvas.

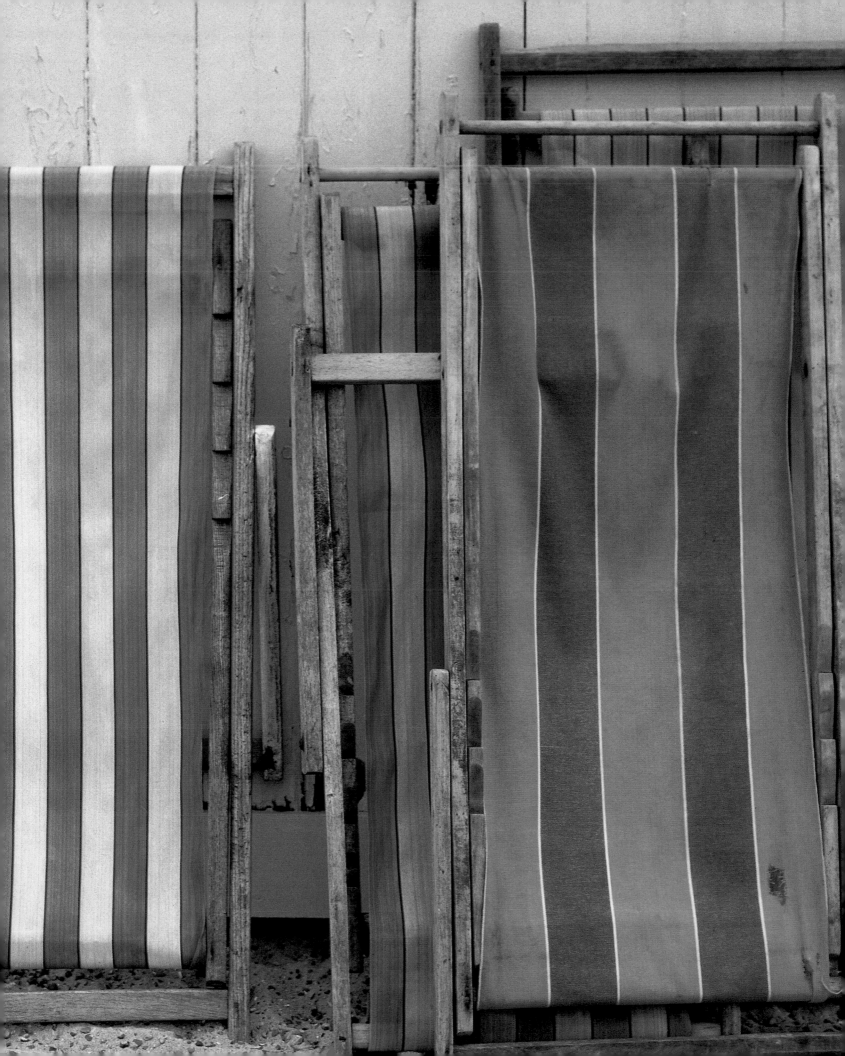

wood

chairs

tables

mosaics

shelves

Seaside Furniture

The simple elegance of wood and whitewash is a timeless solution for seaside homes where mismatched pieces of furniture work well against a backdrop of single-colour walls and flooring. One or two well chosen pieces from different periods can blend happily with junk-shop finds and serve as the foundation for a spontaneous and personal look.

Wood cane and wicker all have a warm, tactile quality – distressed director's chairs make wonderful outdoor or indoor seating, while wooden dining tables, rattan side tables, wicker hampers and trunks all help to create the sort of unselfconscious informal arrangements that evoke an easy, natural environment.

Furniture made from reclaimed timber can be elegant as well as kind to the environment, and one way of guaranteeing yourself such an individual product is to patronise the work of young furniture designers who use natural materials such as driftwood in their contemporary pieces. Commissioning a piece of furniture is not necessarily expensive, and being involved in the whole process, perhaps even specifying the materials and giving pointers to the possible design, is bound

Above: *Transform a nest of tables, purchased in a junk shop, with a layer of seashells. The long razor shells make a perfect edging.*

Left: *Paint a simple metal tabletop with a shell design then wash over the top to give a faded look. Varnish the surface to protect it.*

Right: *Reclaimed timber makes a wonderfully chunky cupboard. Leave the original weatherworn tones of the wood or paint it in bright primary colours.*

Above: *This half-chair, half-sculpture, made from driftwood and fencing, suits this outdoor setting but would look equally striking in a spacious modern interior.*

Below: *The subtle shades of worn painted timbers blend beautifully. To achieve this effect on new paintwork sand back to the wood in areas.*

Left: *This elegant Edwardian-style structure is a windbreak-and-awning in one. It rolls up for easy transport.*

Right: *Director's chairs are the upmarket version of the traditional folding deck chair. They are stylish enough to use indoors.*

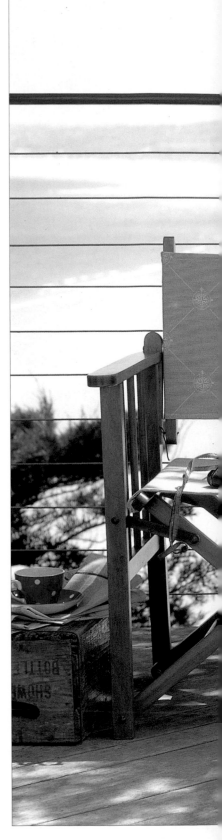

to increase your appreciation of a piece as well as giving you the satisfaction of supporting individual artisans.

Mosaic makes a wonderful surface on furniture and the palette of colours in this art is exquisite. Either commission a mosaic artist to fashion a pictorial design for you or choose something much more simple and use the technique to create your own piece.

If you are an amateur carpenter, then rough wooden pallets can come into their own without too much difficulty – craft them into interesting bedheads and pretty shelves. Search

Below: *Wicker chairs also look equally good indoors or out. Add a large comfortable cushion embroidered with a nautical motif.*

Above: *The reclaimed timbers in this striking wardrobe have been simply used as they are, complete with nails sticking out.*

Left: *This unusual kitchen cupboard has impressive cathedral-style decorative doors. The wooden shelves look right, and are also very practical.*

Right: *Even a grandfather-style clock can be made from odd pieces of wood, giving a new twist to an old look.*

salvage yards, junk shops and antique markets for interesting pieces of furniture that can be renovated. Just strip away any previous coats of paint or varnish, then oil or wax the wood. Finish them off with a wash of water-based paint for a matt distressed effect, or apply a wash of white or tinted paint to produce a faded chalky finish. Alternatively, you could apply sea-greens, blues and soft reds with their cheerful appeal reminiscent of faded beach houses, boats and fishing nets.

To enliven tired wicker furniture, paint it pure brilliant white – this is most definitely a colour that will remind you of seashore verandahs and the simple, clean lines of beach huts. You can find old Lloyd loom chairs and other creaking wicker pieces in junk shops or at car boot sales.

Stack old tea chests, open ends facing out, for an instant storage unit, or turn upside-down for a makeshift table. In addition, you can use their wood to craft a small cupboard.

Flotsam storage: *packing-crate shelves*

These charmingly rustic shelves are created from a cast-off pallet. Pallets can be picked up easily and very cheaply from timber merchants, or you might even find an abandoned one for free in a skip or industrial dustbin. The charm of these shelves is that they have a rather naive quality, so there's no need to be worried if the edges are a bit uneven and wonky – that's all part of the effect. To finish the shelves off, wash them with a diluted emulsion paint in the colour scheme of your choice: try strong Mediterranean colours for a child's bedroom or a bathroom or a soft grey-blue for a sophisticated touch of the American east coast. The end result is the ideal storage solution for toiletries in the bathroom, an array of spices in the kitchen, or seashore finds such as shells and pebbles in a child's room.

YOU WILL NEED:
- **Pallet or orange box**
- **Ruler**
- **Pencil**
- **Saw**
- **Wood glue**
- **Hammer**
- **Nails**
- **Sandpaper**
- **Length of square-edged dowel**
- **Drill (optional)**
- **String (optional)**

1 Decide on what size you want your shelves to be. Measure and cut the shelf and back to the same size from the pallet or orange box. Saw two small pieces for the side sections.

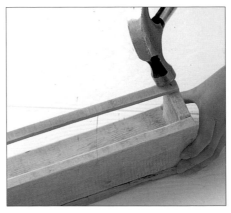

2 Run a line of strong wood glue down the back edge of the base of the shelf. Press the two pieces of wood firmly together to create a right angle. Leave to dry thoroughly.

3 Insert the end-pieces into the right angles at either end of the shelf and hammer three nails in each side to fix firmly in place.

4 Sand the wood down to give a smooth surface as a key for the paint.

5 Take the length of dowel and fix it in position with nails to form a rail across the front of the shelf.

6 For another style of shelf, drill a hole through each end-piece and thread a piece of string through, knotting the string at each end to secure.

Nautical seating: *string and driftwood*

Transform a simple chair into something quite special by binding it with string, attaching pieces of driftwood collected from the beach. Awkward joins are decorated with strips of flotsam and jetsam and two "horns" give the finishing effect to the chair back. Making or changing furniture is just a matter of using what is to hand. String is hardwearing, cheap and gives furniture a tactile quality. Other decorations for the chair could include shells incorporated into the design instead of driftwood, or perhaps a piece of coral to add colour. Try to view furniture as a work of art rather than a functional object, and adapt your chair to suit your mood. Tables, shelves, stools and cupboards can all be adorned with beachcombing finds – it really is just a matter of gathering pieces from the sea-front together and making them work as a harmonious whole.

YOU WILL NEED:	
• **Jute or garden string**	• **Fine gauge fishermen's netting (optional)**
• **Scissors**	• **Staple gun and staples (optional)**
• **Glue gun and sticks**	
• **Chair**	
• **Pieces of driftwood**	

1 Take the ball of string, cut it into manageable lengths and roll these into small balls.

2 Glue the end of a ball of string firmly to the top of the chair to secure the start. You will need to do this each time you begin a new ball.

3 Run a thin line of glue up the back of the chair to secure the string while you are working. Pull the string taut while you wrap it around the chair, making sure that it doesn't overlap and twist.

4 To decorate the struts on the back of the chair, wrap the string over a bunch of driftwood pieces at the join. Wind one way to secure it, then wind back again. ➤

5 *Make two criss-cross patterns along the middle of the chair strut to decorate. Hold them in place with glue.*

6 *To fix the driftwood pieces to the top of the chair, apply some glue along them.*

7 *Position the driftwood pieces on the chair as desired.*

8 *Secure the driftwood pieces in place with string. To finish off, knot the string and bind it underneath.*

9 *As a variation, you could upholster the seat of the chair with netting. Take a piece of fishermen's netting and fold it in half.*

10 *Secure the netting firmly to the underneath of the chair seat with a staple gun.*

Seascape colours: *mosaic table*

This mosaic table provides a stunning focal point for any room. It evokes fresh sea breezes sweeping in off the water, and it would work equally well inside or out of doors. Mosaics are currently experiencing a tremendous revival and they provide an opportunity to create wonderful designs, from the simple swirls shown here to intricately decorated panels. Glass mosaic squares come in a huge range of colours, from muted matt shades of grey-greens and blues to searing primaries and shiny metallics. Provided you keep the shape and design simple, the whole process can be completed by even the most inexperienced of mosaic creators.

YOU WILL NEED:
- **Piece of plywood**
- **Jigsaw**
- **Sharp knife**
- **PVA glue**
- **Paintbrushes**
- **Pencil**
- **Protective goggles**
- **Tile nippers**
- **Vitreous glass squares, in various colours**
- **Cement-based tile adhesive powder**
- **Soft brush**
- **Plant sprayer**
- **Cloths**
- **Rubber gloves**
- **Fine sandpaper**

1 Cut the plywood to the desired shape for your table. Scour it with a sharp knife and prime it with a coat of diluted PVA glue. Leave to dry thoroughly.

2 Draw swirls radiating from the centre for the design on the table pictured here, or create your own design.

3 Wearing protective goggles, use tile nippers to cut white glass squares into quarters. Use different densities of white to add interest to the design.

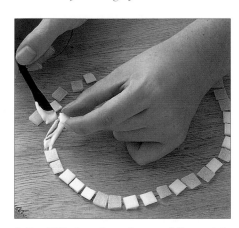

4 Put PVA glue along the pencil line swirls, then position the white glass on them, smooth side up.

5 Select your colours for the areas between the white lines. Here, browns and sand colours form the edge while blues, greens and whites form the central areas. Spread out your selected colours to see if the combinations work.

6 Cut your chosen squares into quarters, using the tile nippers and wearing protective goggles.

7 *Glue the central pieces to the tabletop with PVA glue.*

8 *To finish off the edge, glue pieces around the border of the table. Leave to dry thoroughly overnight.*

9 *Sprinkle dry cement-based tile adhesive powder over the mosaic surface and spread it over using a soft brush. Make sure that all the spaces between the tile pieces are filled.*

10 *Spray water over the mosaic, making sure that all the cement is wet. Wipe away any excess with a cloth.*

11 *Mix some cement-based tile adhesive with water and, wearing rubber gloves, rub it into the edges of the table with your fingers. Leave to dry overnight.*

12 *Rub off any excess cement with fine sandpaper and polish the table with a soft cloth.*

Duckboarding: *bath mat*

Duckboarding immediately brings to mind boats, marinas and luxurious days spent beside a pool with the sound of splashing water in the background. This duckboard bath mat is made from strips of wood and can either be used within the shower or as a mat on which to step out of the bath. If you are feeling even more adventurous, then create a whole floor in a similar fashion, but position the slats a little closer together. This would make a highly original surface for a bathroom, and coming out of the bath to feel the smooth wood underfoot is a treat most would enjoy. Use a hardwood to withstand water and make sure that it is treated with a water-resistant matt yachting varnish when finished to help preserve it.

YOU WILL NEED:
- **Hardwood strips, 5 x 2.5 cm (2 x 1 in)**
- **Saw**
- **Sandpaper**
- **Ruler**
- **Pencil**
- **Bradawl**
- **Wood glue**
- **Brass screws**
- **Screwdriver**
- **Matt yachting varnish**
- **Paintbrush**

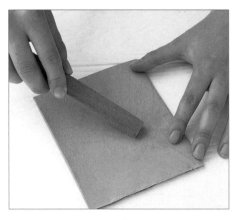

1 Decide on the size of your bath mat. Allowing for 2.5 cm (1 in) between slats, work out how many slats you need. Cut the wood to size. Sand the ends of the pieces.

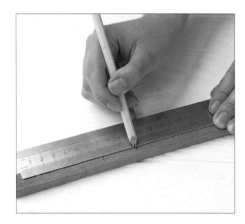

2 Cut two lengths of wood to act as the cross-pieces on to which all the slats are fixed. Mark them at regular intervals where the slats will be.

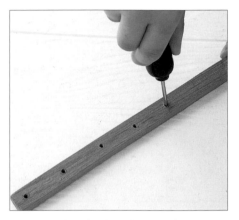

3 Using a bradawl, make holes for the brass screws in the centre of the marks.

4 Mark on the back of each end of the wooden slats where the cross-pieces will go. Place a small amount of wood glue on these marks.

5 Position the cross-pieces on top of the slats, matching up all the marks. Fix them in place with brass screws. Finish the mat off with a coat of yachting varnish.

Sea-weathered effects: *director's chair*

If you're one of those people who dislikes the fresh, clean look of a newly-painted surface, then this ageing treatment is the one for you to try. It instantly transforms furniture from new to old, imbuing pieces with an interesting weathered quality in next to no time, albeit at an accelerated pace, thus allowing it to blend into its surroundings. Getting away from a beautifully flat, pristine paint surface and acquiring an old, worn look makes an object more comfortable to live with and more relaxing to look at. Here, by using an ageing technique, a basic director's chair is given a whole new dimension. Changing the vivid cover for one with a soft, rather washed-out stripe also adds to the overall effect of a comfortable seaside life.

YOU WILL NEED:
- **Director's chair**
- **Scrubbing brush**
- **Bucket**
- **Soapy water**
- **Cloth**
- **Masking tape**
- **White candle**
- **Emulsion paint, in pale blue and white**
- **Paint pot**
- **Paintbrushes**
- **Sandpaper**
- **Matt varnish**

1 Remove the cover from the chair and rub off any excess dirt from the frame with the scrubbing brush.

2 Scrub the chair clean with the scrubbing brush and soapy water.

3 Wipe the chair down with a clean, dry cloth and then leave it to dry thoroughly.

4 Put masking tape over all the metal attachments on the chair.

5 *Rub the chair with a candle to deposit wax on the surface, concentrating on the edges and corners. The heavier the wax deposit, the more distressed it will look.*

6 *Dilute the pale blue emulsion paint in the proportion 3:1 with water in the paint pot or bucket.*

7 *Apply a coat of paint all over the chair. Leave to dry thoroughly.*

8 *Rub over the paint with sandpaper to reveal the wood underneath, then rub the chair all over with the candle again.*

9 *Dilute the white paint 3:1 with water.*

10 *Apply a coat of white paint over the chair. Leave to dry thoroughly.*

11 *Rub over the paint with sandpaper to reveal the wood in some parts, and the blue paint in others.*

12 *Seal the chair using a matt varnish to protect the surface. When dry, replace the chair cover.*

Sea-washed: *simple shelving*

Create a stunning hanging shelf using a single floorboard. Wood stainer and a wash of white emulsion give the surface a distressed finish. Knotted rope is then the perfect partner to blend with the distressed wood and give a real nautical air. Neutral displays look wonderful when decorated with simple twigs, strings of seashells and feathers, all gathered from the beach. If you are looking for something more vibrant, just paint or stain the shelves in a brighter Mediterranean colour, or you could use warm blues and grey-greens to create a shelf more akin to an Atlantic coastline.

YOU WILL NEED:
- **Floorboard or plank of wood**
- **Pencil**
- **Ruler**
- **Saw**
- **Drill**
- **Sandpaper**
- **Wood stainer**
- **Cloths**
- **White emulsion paint**
- **Paintbrush**
- **Matt varnish (optional)**
- **4 lengths of rope**
- **Masking tape**
- **Glue gun and sticks**

1 Cut the floorboard or wooden plank into three pieces of equal length, depending on how long you want your shelves to be. Each piece should be 2.5 cm (1 in) wider than the next.

2 Using a pencil and ruler, measure and mark two holes at each end of the three shelf pieces. They should all align where you want the rope to go through.

3 Drill holes through the marks you have made on each of the three pieces of wood. Rub down the wood with sandpaper to make sure it is smooth.

4 Wipe the stainer evenly over the pieces of shelving using a clean cloth. Leave to dry thoroughly.

5 Dilute the white paint in the proportion 4:1 with water and apply a thin wash over the shelves.

6 Using a soft, absorbent cloth, rub away most of the white paint to leave a distressed look.

➤

7 Varnish the wood with a matt varnish, if required, to prevent staining once in use.

8 Take two lengths of rope and wind masking tape around the ends. Knot one end of each rope and thread the other ends through the two holes on one end of the widest shelf. Mark two positions on the rope at the desired height on the middle shelf and tie a knot.

9 Thread the rope through the middle shelf. Mark two positions with masking tape at the height you want the top shelf to hang. Tie a secure knot.

10 Thread the rope through the top shelf. Using a glue gun, glue all the knots to the holes to secure the shelves.

11 Knot the rope firmly at the top of the third shelf as shown, and glue it firmly in place.

Rustic planks: *pallet headboard*

The next time you see a pallet abandoned on the roadside, don't just walk past it – take a closer look at it and consider whether it is worth taking it home to fashion into a wondrous piece of furniture. Here, a pallet was rescued and transformed into a headboard for a bed. It could equally well have ended up as a cupboard, shelves or even a tabletop. With a quick lick of paint, the crude wood becomes an object which would be equally at home in a modern apartment or a beach hut by the sea. The pallet retains its natural roughness due to the different widths of the planks and nail holes but the end effect is one of charm and tranquillity.

YOU WILL NEED:
- **Pallet**
- **Hammer**
- **Ruler**
- **Pencil**
- **Saw**
- **Nails**
- **Coarse grade sandpaper**
- **White emulsion paint**
- **Paint pot**
- **Paintbrush**
- **Matt varnish (optional)**

1 Remove the nails and struts of wood from the pallet.

2 Decide on the size of the headboard, then measure and cut the wood to size.

3 Make a support for the headboard by nailing four pieces of wood together, plus a piece fixed centrally for stability.

4 Nail the varying widths of wood to this frame to form the front of the headboard. Sand down all the wood to prevent splinters forming.

5 Paint the headboard with two coats of watered-down white paint so that the grain shows through. If desired, finish the headboard with a coat of matt varnish.

Shoreline Details

lamps

screens

mirrors

candles

pictures

frames

pots

trimmings

tie-backs

blinds

driftwood

shells

In a simple interior, details add a personal note and breathe life into a room. Make the most of *objets trouvés* brought back as souvenirs from trips to the seaside. Collecting shells and pebbles on a shingly beach is even more addictive if you know that you are going to use them later. Even the sculptural shapes of humble driftwood reappear in the home as functional objects, witty and very modern. The roughness of rope, jute and raffia gives yet another note of character and texture that is strongly reminiscent of ships and the sea. Picture and mirror frames can be decorated in a variety of ways – covered with shells for a Victorian look, or with a striking blue-and-white china mosaic improvised from broken or chipped tiles and crockery. A plain wooden picture frame is also very typical of seashore style. Distress the wood first, then glue on small fish or model boats picked up from a fishing-tackle or toy shop.

Shoreline Details

Natural treasures such as seashells, starfish, stones, coral and driftwood can be bought in shops, but that somehow misses the point and is, besides, very damaging to the environment. If you cannot find the shells you need, then use only those you know to be by-products of the fishing industry, such as mussel or oyster shells. Shells and coral on sale in craft shops have been harvested when the animal is still alive – this is why they look so uniformly shiny and free from imperfection. Excessive harvesting has driven some species to the brink of extinction.

The delight of discovery is one of the earliest and most enduring of life's pleasures, and it gives found objects a special meaning. Knowing on which beach you unearthed your prize enchances the delight of a found object. Most of us return from holiday or weekend breaks with pockets and rucksacks stuffed with finds. Instead of simply discarding

Above: *Fill plain glass containers with creamy white shells and sea-smoothed pebbles.*

Left: *Use shells, stones and other* objets trouvés *for a subtle display that is pleasing to the eye.*

Right: *For a quick and easy blind, simply fringe the edge of a raffia mat. Add a small piece of driftwood as a blind pull.*

Left: *Enliven a plain picture frame with gilded seashore motifs.*

Right: *To distress a wooden frame, apply crackle glaze over a layer of paint. When the glaze has dried, paint in a different colour and the bottom colour will show through.*

Below: *Make a fish skeleton out of strips of driftwood, with a rivet for the eye. Glue on to a large piece of wood and hang on the wall.*

such mementos, you can easily incorporate them into your surroundings and enjoy their elemental qualities and associations long after your return.

Accessories and soft furnishings form an integral part of interior design, so use them to reflect your personal tastes and surround yourself with things that you like. Think of rooms without pictures, flowers or decorative objects of any kind – they can be beautiful spaces but they lack character and a sense of being inhabited. Give your decorative ideas pride of place and they will attract and hold onlookers' attention.

To stamp your personality on a room, you could simply adorn a brown paper lampshade with a fringe of pebbles and set it at a jaunty angle, or decorate an existing plain mirror with a host of seashore finds – the end result will grace anyone's bathroom and reflect back every bit of available light. Use souvenirs from seaside strolls and fishing trips to make a decorative window screen to diffuse the streaming summer sun or to disguise a less-than-picturesque view.

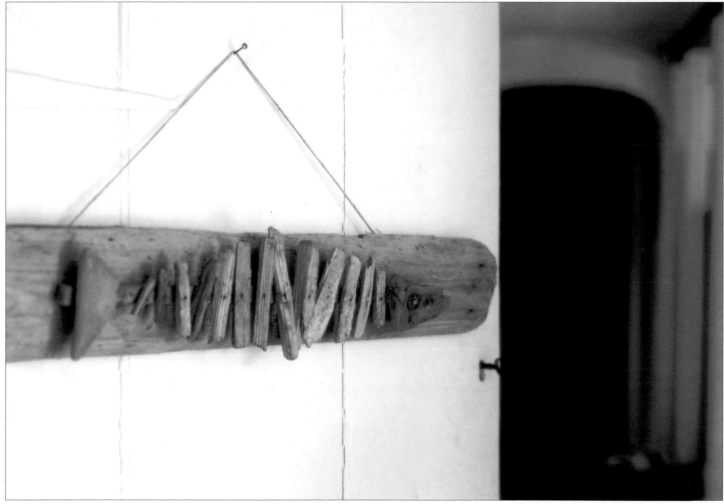

The scope for decoration is boundless and materials are plentiful and free. Found objects can form an integral part of any natural display. Play colour against colour, texture against texture. Turn simple strips of driftwood into quirky candlesticks complete with feathered hands, and experiment with different arrangements and locations to keep the effect fresh, spontaneous and lively.

Above: *Cover a mirror frame with a rich collection of shells and coral, glued in position.*

Below: *Mediterranean pots make a strong statement in a garden or sitting room. The soft blues are reminiscent of sea and sky.*

Above: *This beautifully simple laundry bag is made of white linen, decorated with a few delicate shells.*

Right: *Broken or chipped tiles and crockery can find new life as the basis for a mosaic to decorate a box, or the frame of a mirror. Here, toning shades of blue evoke a seashore theme, as do the contrasting white starfish shapes.*

Sea-tumbled trimmings: *pebble lampshade*

Bring a touch of class and a quirky seaside style to a simple brown paper lampshade. Using pebbles worn smooth by sea waters and picked up from the beach, you can create a work of art that is truly individual. All natural materials work harmoniously together, so pebbles and raffia combined with brown paper are absolutely perfect. Here, a curvaceous metal frame adds a jaunty seaside angle to the shade – an additional option would be to bind the metal stem with string to give it an even more natural feel.

YOU WILL NEED:
- **Raffia**
- **Small pebbles**
- **Glue gun and sticks**
- **Paper lampshade**
- **Scissors**

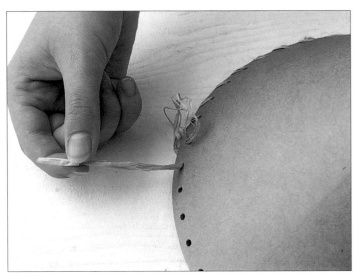

1 Thread the raffia through the top and bottom edges of the lampshade instead of ribbon.

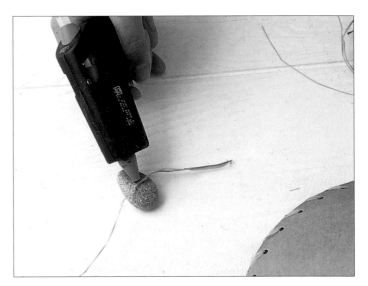

2 Pull thin strips of raffia apart and position the pieces on the pebbles. Glue them together.

3 Tie the raffia around the pebbles in neat knots.

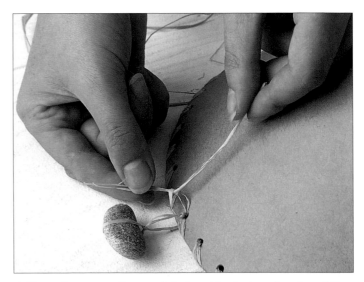

4 Hang the stones all around the lampshade, knotting the pebbles in place. Trim the loose ends of the raffia.

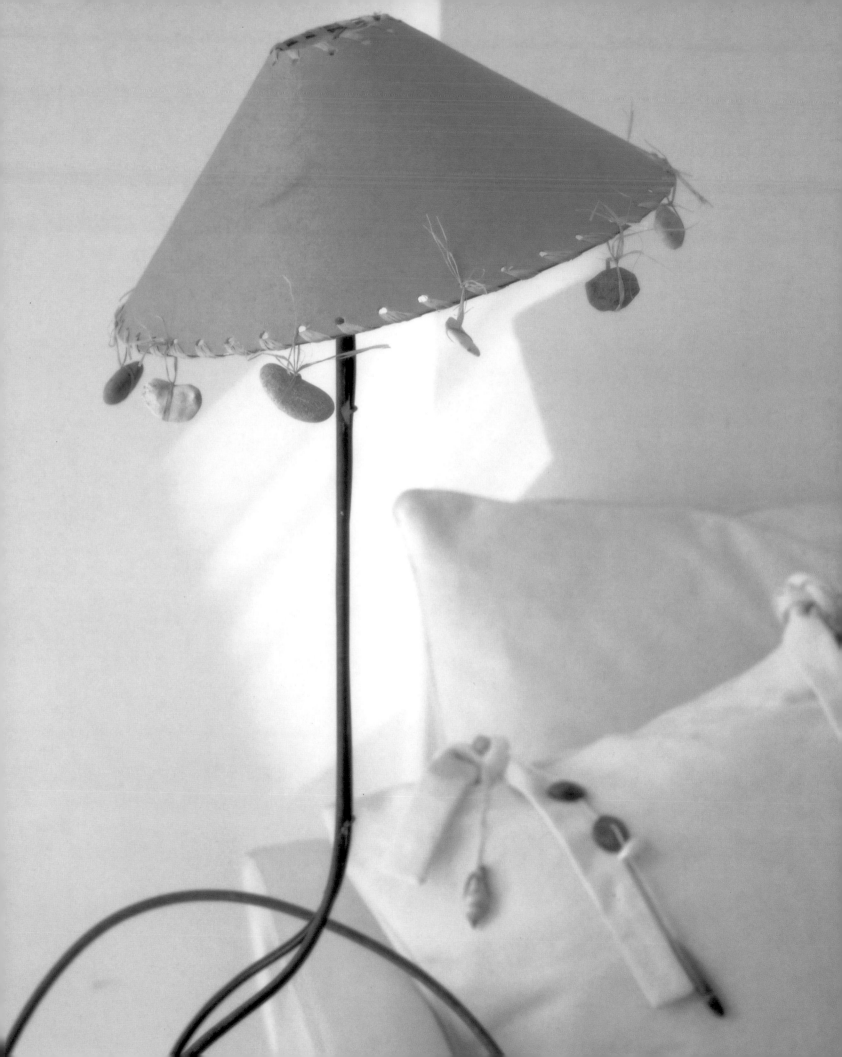

Sand and shells: *shelf edging*

Make the perfect seaside setting by introducing a shelf edging that is not only reminiscent of the waves of the sea in its shape but is coated with a fine spray of sand and decorated with the prettiest of shells. This makes an ideal bathroom or bedroom addition and also works very effectively in any kitchen area. Living rooms could benefit too, as the alcoves beside a chimney breast can be fitted with four shelves either side and each shelf could be decorated in a different design. Small stones could be used for one, a collection of wonderful coloured glass worn smooth by the action of the sea could make another, or shells, as here – there are many options. A more ornate design such as rolling waves could also be used, but this would need to be cut with a jigsaw. If you don't want to go to the trouble of cutting your own shaped shelf edging, there are many available in a variety of designs, all in untreated timber so you can simply buy the edging, paint it and decorate it as you see appropriate.

YOU WILL NEED:
- **Piece of plywood**
- **Dinner plate**
- **Pencil**
- **Saw or jigsaw**
- **Fine sandpaper**
- **White emulsion paint**
- **Paintbrushes**
- **PVA glue or spray mount**
- **Silver sand**
- **Glue gun and sticks**
- **Shells**

1 Take the plywood and, using the edge of a dinner plate, mark a scalloped edging. Use a side plate or even a saucer for smaller edging.

2 Using a saw or jigsaw, cut out your shelf-edge design and sand the edges smooth with fine sandpaper.

3 Apply a coat of white emulsion paint to the edging. Leave to dry thoroughly.

4 Apply a coat of PVA glue to the edging, or spray it with spray mount, to cover the surface evenly.

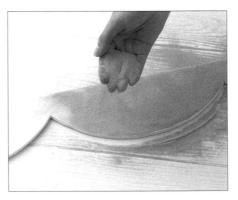

5 While still tacky, sprinkle a fine layer of silver sand to cover the whole of the shelf. It doesn't matter if it goes a little patchy as this is part of the charm. Leave to dry.

6 Using a glue gun, glue shells on to the edging to make an attractive design.

Seaside finds: *window screen*

This is an ideal screen for any window which isn't overlooked, as its main purpose is to act as a fascinating decorative foil. It would make a lovely hanging in the watery world of the bathroom, in an attic bedroom or in a small window in a hallway. It is an individual way of displaying seashore finds, such as worn glass, shells and stones and newer items such as fishing floats, weights and lures (with their hooks removed). Everything is fixed on with near-invisible fishing line so the screen appears to be floating in mid-air within the window space. The more you gaze at it, the more the image of the sea is brought to mind.

YOU WILL NEED:
- **Seaside finds, such as glass, shells and fishing tackle**
- **Fishing line**
- **Glue gun and sticks (optional)**
- **Bradawl**
- **Piece of dowel**
- **Hooks and rings**

1 On a flat surface, lay out your selection of seaside objects in a design of your choice.

2 Tie the objects on to lengths of fishing line, either making holes and knotting them or fixing them on with a glue gun.

3 Using a bradawl, make holes in the dowel at regular intervals and insert hooks.

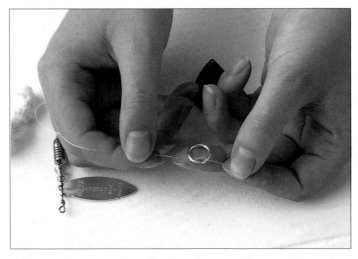

4 Fix the rings on to the ends of the decorated lines and hang them from the hooks on the dowel.

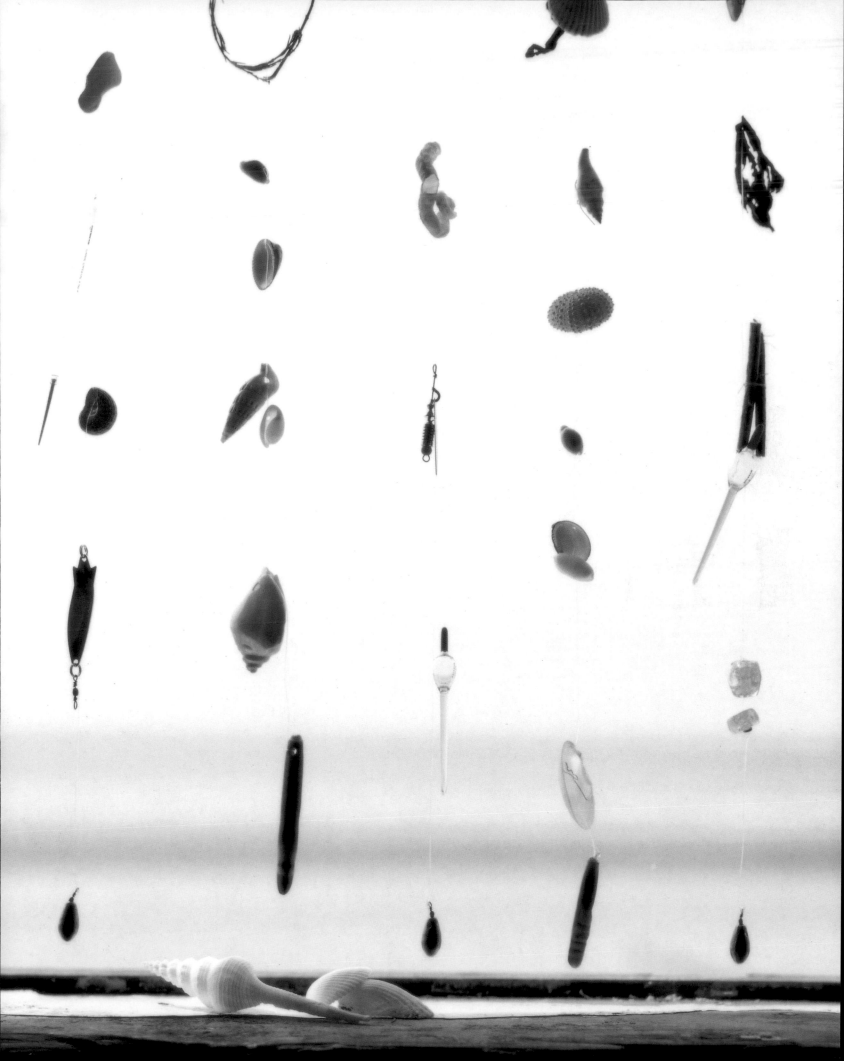

Set sail: *framed boat picture*

Dress up an old frame and create your very own work of art, without even needing to be able to draw. Again, it is largely a matter of searching the beach or seashore for interesting pebbles, seaweed and pieces of driftwood. The recycled picture frame used here works particularly well as it has a driftwood appearance to begin with. These types of frames are fairly widely available both in natural wood and woods which have been washed with a soft grey-blue or grey-green pigment. Failing that, you can always buy a simple wooden frame or buy a stretcher (these are simple wooden struts in varying sizes which slot together to make an instant frame available from art shops). This can either be painted, or a selection of driftwood could be glued around the edge for a particularly interesting finish.

YOU WILL NEED:
- **String**
- **Scissors**
- **Picture frame in recycled timber**
- **Thick card**
- **Fibre pot, from garden centre**
- **Pebble**
- **Glue gun and sticks**
- **Seaweed**

1 Cut a length of string and wind this around the top and bottom of the frame to make a casual yet interesting design. Tie to secure. Cut a piece of card to act as a backing.

2 For the boat picture, tear the fibre pot into small pieces to make the sail shapes. ➤

3 *Lay out your pebble and sails to make sure they balance.*

4 *Arrange the pebble and sails on the backing card and glue them firmly in position.*

5 *Experiment to see where the seaweed looks most attractive.*

6 *Glue the seaweed into position.*

Left: *The natural beauty of driftwood is an invaluable inspiration. The texture and colour provide practical ideas for decorating frames, while the strange, sculpted shapes of branches that have been battered by the elements can be re-created in miniature for a naturally abstract picture.*

Seaside views: *shell mirror*

This is the perfect way either to dress up an existing mirror or to create a very special one of your own. It makes a wonderful gift and all sea-loving friends are bound to be enchanted by the mixture of sand and seashells. Any shape of mirror is suitable for this treatment which is a beautiful addition to any bathroom, bedroom or hallway; rectangular and oval mirrors are especially effective and interesting. When finished, position the shell-encrusted mirror on the wall so it reflects every patch of blue there is and allows sunlight to bounce off it and light up the room.

YOU WILL NEED:
- **Tape measure**
- **Mirror**
- **Piece of hardboard**
- **Hanging hook**
- **Glue gun and sticks**
- **PVA glue**
- **Sand**
- **Paper**
- **Card (optional)**
- **Shells – scallop, mussels, razors, smaller shells, drilled, and tiny shells**
- **Twine**
- **Tweezers**
- **Seaweed**

1 Measure the mirror and cut a piece of hardboard slightly larger all around to allow for the decorative border. Attach a hanging hook to the back of the hardboard.

2 Attach the mirror to the hardboard using a glue gun.

3 Coat the hardboard border with PVA glue and, using the paper as a funnel, sprinkle it with sand to create a seaside background.

4 If required, fix a piece of card in the centre of the top of the mirror to support a central shell. ➤

5 *Decide upon your design and position the central shell and some mussel shells on the top.*

6 *Position some mussel shells around the edge of the frame and fix them securely with a glue gun.*

7 *Thread smaller shells along twine to fix a length around the edge of the border.*

8 *Glue tiny shells into position inside the outer row of mussel shells.*

9 *Glue another layer of mussel shells on to the inner edge, fixing them to the surface of the mirror itself.*

10 *Glue razor shells in place on the bottom edge of the mirror to form a "V" shape.*

11 *Using tweezers, position tiny shells in between all the edging shells to cover any of the mirror under the edge. Glue in place.*

12 *To finish, position strands of seaweed where required and glue them in place with the glue gun.*

Nautical knots: *curtain tie-back*

Take a tip from able-bodied seamen and create a stunning tie-back from a length of rope and a simple slip stitch. The only technical skill required is a basic knowledge of how to knit. The tassel is secured by "whipping", a well-known seafaring term for binding ropes together using twine or string. Fasten the tie-back with a simple cleat decorated with a single pebble, to give an even greater seafaring feel. This type of curtain treatment looks marvellous when used with cream calico or linen fabric – muslin would look beautiful too, but you might need to use a finer gauge of rope.

YOU WILL NEED:
- **1–1.5 m (1–1½ yd) length of rope**
- **Dressmaker's pin**
- **Jute string**
- **Scissors**

1 Tie a knot in the end of a length of rope. Work a chain stitch in the rope; this is the same technique as casting on with one needle and one finger for knitting, i.e. make two loops.

2 Thread one loop through the other loop, tightening as you go.

3 To make the tassel, unravel the end of the rope and fluff it out by running a dressmaker's pin down the unravelled sections to separate out the fibres.

4 Bind jute string around the rope end using a whip knot. Make a loop at the bottom and top ends of the string, leaving a tail of about 8 cm (3 in) at the bottom end.

5 From the top, start to whip around the rope with the string, leaving both loops visible. Whip as closely and as tightly as possible, keeping the string bound closely together and working with an even tension.

6 To finish, thread the string through the lower loop and pull the loop at the other end. As you pull harder, the other end of the string pulls through. Snip off the ends of the string to neaten.

Sculpted by the waves: *driftwood candlestick*

Create a truly free expressionistic candlestick by amalgamating various items from the beach, such as birds' feathers and bits of wood or fishing tackle. The end result will delight all onlookers and it radiates a certain spirit of its own. Remember, though, that lit candles must never be left unattended – and especially so in this instance with driftwood and feathers providing the base. Because of the sculptural nature of this particular piece, it could happily stand on its own as an art object without being lit.

YOU WILL NEED:

- **2–3 pieces of driftwood**
- **Glue gun and sticks**
- **Florist's wire**
- **2 feathers**
- **Craft knife**
- **Candle**

1 Use two or three pieces of driftwood to form a pleasing candlestick base. Using a glue gun, fix the driftwood pieces together.

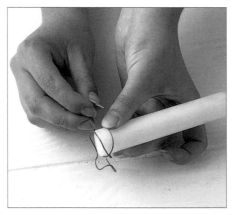

2 When dry, bind a piece of wire around the cross section and fashion it into two candelabra-shaped arms.

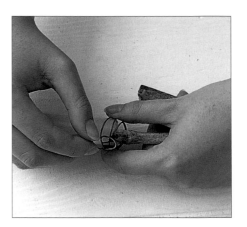

3 Fix the feathers on to the arms by placing a dot of glue on the ends of the wires and inserting these into the quills.

4 Using a craft knife, make a small hole in the end of a candle to stabilize it within the candle holder.

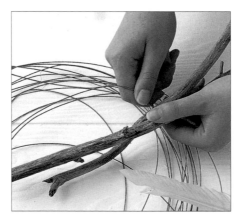

5 Cut a shortish length of wire and wind it around the base of the candle, to make the candle holder.

6 Insert this wire holder into the top of the candlestick. Position the candle, anchoring it in place with a tiny piece of driftwood, and secure it by tightening up the wire. Do not let the candle burn down to its driftwood anchor.

Sea Accessories

ceramics

books

boats

glassware

china

boxes

lanterns

games

pots

placenames

trays

bottles

Accessories can add colour and style to every part of your home. Create a series of still-life effects within the home by rearranging favourite accessories to suit your mood, the season and the occasion. In the daytime, place decorative glasses and bottles in vivid blues and greens on a sunny windowsill so that they catch the light. Display cheerfully spotted blue cups and saucers on a kitchen shelf or dresser. For dinner guests, bring out shell candles and hurricane lamps, and carry on the seashore theme by laying the table with pebble place names. Give a fresh look to traditional crafts by painting plain glass and china with your own seashore motifs, or decorating trays and boxes with fish or shell découpage in bright modern colours. The ideal solution for a collection of small disparate objects is to bring them all together in a sand garden, which you can revise and add to after each visit to the seaside.

boats

ceramics

china

boxes

glassware

Sea
Accessories

Seaside and country walks can yield all manner of unusual and beautiful objects discarded by humankind and nature alike. Sculptural branches and twigs, pine cones, acorns, seeds and seed heads, a wide variety of leaves, seaweed, old chandlers' rope, pebbles, starfish and seashells can all be gathered together to form the basis of your craft materials. Once collected, they can be transformed into a wealth of attractive and original decorative objects which make wonderful accessories for the home.

Other decorative ideas can be crafted from everyday items found just about anywhere. For example, if you've got a simple tea box, just paint it in the colour of your choice, then decorate it with a cornucopia of shells, or turn glasses and vases into display cases overflowing with seashore finds. Likewise, you could decorate plain carafes, storage jars and white china with stunning seaside designs, or make a striking statement on a windowsill with a row of coloured glass and antique bottles.

Above: *Delight your guests with personalized pebble place names.*

Left: *This cast concrete seagull, found at a car boot sale, is a witty addition to the most conventional mantelpiece or shelf. The shoreline pebbles reinforce the nautical theme of the display.*

Right: *Set the breakfast table with an ethnic embroidered napkin and scarlet geraniums, and imagine you are on a Greek island.*

Above: Tin lanterns are imported now from many countries. Mix different shapes and sizes for magical summer evenings.

Below: To make lovely individual candles, place a nightlight in each mussel shell, then fill the shell with melted candlewax.

By using your surroundings as inspiration you can achieve quite impressive results with the materials available. To turn a plain garden seed box into a painted aquarium with exotic fish floating over the surface, cut out pictures of marine animals from a book or magazine and apply them to the box's surface using a découpage technique. Découpage is also ideal for screens, walls or even pieces of furniture, and images such as birds, shells, lighthouses and boats can all be used to evoke a seashore mood.

Inexpensive woven baskets, available in garden centres, make ideal containers for kitchens, bathrooms or bedrooms. They are already decorative and can usually be made even more so by adding lengths of tiny shell necklaces in a zig-zag design. Found objects can form an integral part of natural displays, as in a sand garden with a rugged frame constructed from reclaimed timber and filled with flotsam from the beach. A tiny piece of driftwood can be used to craft a small sailing boat while a simple shell and garden pot becomes a pretty sailing vessel.

Right: The flames from floating candles cast soft reflections in the water, reminiscent of night-time fishing boats at sea.

Far right: Glue small shells on to the covers of colourful notebooks and decorate a terracotta pot to match.

Creating special items for the home can be as economical as it is satisfying, and there is often no need to visit specialist craft suppliers when focusing on a seashore theme – use pieces of cast-off garden twine or household string to make shoals of fish and jaunty anchors on hand-made notepaper and chunky bookcovers.

Group together old bottles found on the shore and place a candle in each to illuminate an informal supper. Another wonderful idea is to make your own lanterns from simple tin cans. Remove the labels and place a piece of wood in each can for a brace. Using a sharp implement such as a bradawl, make tiny pin pricks in a design all over the surface. When you light your lantern, the candlelight will flicker through.

Right: *Decorate a window box or planter with mussel shells and fill with plants in toning colours.*

Above: *Stitch rows of shells on to a wicker basket for a beautiful contrast of texture.*

Left: *Gift-wrap herbs or small presents in fabric bags tied with string and decorated with shells and driftwood.*

Right: *This elaborate outdoor display uses candles, starfish, sand and driftwood to dramatic effect.*

Marineware: *painted carafe*

Add another dimension to a plain glass carafe by painting stunning seaside scenes directly on to the glass. Pieces of seaweed, shell images and starfish are all suitable images. If you want to create a special seaside setting for a particular dinner party, simply paint on the images with white emulsion and they can be washed off at the end of the evening. Alternatively, use glass paint and create a range of stylish natural glassware in tune with a seashore way of life. Don't restrict yourself to just one carafe – make a display of matching glassware with a variety of glasses and jugs in all shapes and sizes.

YOU WILL NEED:
- **Carafe**
- **Lint-free cotton**
- **Methylated spirits**
- **Pencil**
- **Paper**
- **Tracing paper**
- **Masking tape**
- **Carbon paper**
- **Marker pen**
- **White glass paint**
- **Paintbrush**

1 Wipe the surface of the glass with lint-free cotton and methylated spirits to make the surface absolutely clean.

2 Draw up your designs, either using the templates at the back of the book or your own freehand illustrations.

3 Transfer your designs to tracing paper.

4 Using masking tape, stick your designs around the carafe, placing a piece of carbon paper underneath the tracing paper. Draw around the outline with a sharp pen so that the outline is transferred to the glass.

5 Paint the outlines and fill the designs in with white glass paint.

6 Alternatively, place the image inside the carafe or on the other side of the glass and paint the image through the glass.

Dining by the sea: *painted china*

Fine white china is beautiful in its own right but here is a way of injecting colour and adding another dimension to a plain white dinner set. If you are throwing a special dinner party and are committed to pushing the boat out, then embellish additional decorative plates and soup bowls for each setting using emulsion paint – although these items should not be used for food. The paint can be wiped off the next day. However, if you use a ceramic paint, tableware can be decorated permanently. Small images of shells and starfish look delicate, or ring the changes and use one maritime motif around a plate, with each place setting being different. Likewise, if the images are enlarged on a photocopier, then a central image on each plate can look lovely. Experiment with different sizes – just copy each image a few times, then play around with the sizes to see which you find the most pleasing.

YOU WILL NEED:
- **Tracing paper**
- **Pencil**
- **Scissors**
- **China plates and soup bowls**
- **Lint-free cotton**
- **Methylated spirits**
- **Ruler**
- **Carbon paper**
- **Masking tape**
- **Blue ceramic paint**
- **Fine paintbrush**

1 Copy the template from the back of the book on to tracing paper, or make a template of your own design. Cut the shapes out with sharp scissors.

2 Wipe the surface of the plate with lint-free cotton and methylated spirits to make the surface absolutely clean.

3 Find and mark the middle of the plate with a ruler and pencil.

➤

4 *Section the plate into eight equal parts and mark up the eight sections.*

5 *Try various design options with your templates to see which one you find the most pleasing.*

6 *Cut carbon paper into small pieces to fit your templates.*

7 *Place the carbon paper under the template designs on the plate and stick them down firmly with masking tape to secure.*

8 *Trace around the template outlines with a sharp pencil, then remove the tape and templates.*

9 *Paint in the shapes carefully using ceramic paint. Leave to dry thoroughly.*

10 *Mark, trace and paint the design in the centre of the soup bowl.*

11 *Add small dots on the handles of the bowl. Leave to dry thoroughly.*

12 *Remove the pencil marks from the china before using.*

Letters from afar: *notepaper and book*

There is nothing more flattering or personal than receiving notepaper, stationery and notebooks that have been hand-crafted. Making paper is not difficult, but it can be a time-consuming affair. However, it is extremely easy to decorate ready-bought paper, and it is wonderful to incorporate motifs such as anchors or fish, for example, which bring the seaside to mind. Using a pale cream paper and natural string creates a gift that is elegant in its simplicity.

Book

YOU WILL NEED:
- **Thick garden twine**
- **Pieces of driftwood**
- **Glue gun and sticks**
- **Notebook**

1 Tie a piece of thick garden twine to each end of a piece of driftwood. Knot in place.

2 Tie further sticks to the twine to form a line, pulling it taut at the top and bottom.

3 To make the book cover, glue the row of driftwood in position on to the notebook.

4 Tie the pieces of twine at the ends to complete the book.

➤

Envelope and Notepaper

YOU WILL NEED:

- Paper
- Single-hole punch
- PVA glue
- String
- Pieces of driftwood
- Scissors

1 To make the envelope, fold over a piece of paper, leaving a shorter edge to fold down as the flap of the envelope (about one-eighth of the paper).

2 Punch six holes for the string: two on the flap and four on the back of the envelope, as shown.

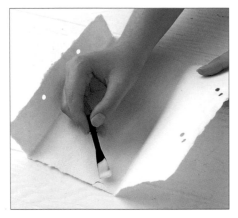

3 Put PVA glue along the sides of the envelope and glue it down.

4 Thread pieces of string through the holes and knot them in place.

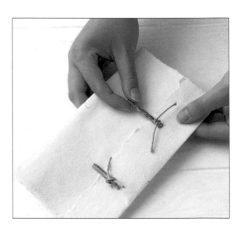

5 Slip pieces of driftwood under the string to decorate.

6 To make the fish for the notepaper, cut a small piece of string and cross the ends over to form a fish shape. Cut a thin strip for the end of the tail. Glue the fish on the paper to secure it.

7 To make the anchor, knot a piece of string in the centre and bend up the ends to form a base. Glue a single piece of driftwood for the upright, then glue everything in place.

Shell-encrusted: *decorative box*

Turn a simple tea box into a special gift with the addition of a little paint and a motif made from shells and driftwood. Once thought to be rather *outré*, shell boxes have now made a big comeback and are considered something to be desired, in a rather kitsch sort of way. Making a shell box is really quite straightforward – just choose a charming selection of bits and pieces and arrange them as you like. Choose a motif that you feel is suitable, such as an urn, crescent, horn or anchor, then draw up the shape and fill it with tiny shells. If you run out of shells, fill the spaces with seeds, beans or pulses. As long as the colouring matches, then anything goes.

YOU WILL NEED:
- **Tea box**
- **Black emulsion paint**
- **Paintbrush**
- **Thick card**
- **Craft knife**
- **Saucer**
- **Small shells**
- **Glue gun and sticks**
- **Pieces of driftwood**
- **Florist's wire**

1 Paint a tea box with an even coat of black emulsion paint. Leave to dry thoroughly.

2 Cut out a crescent from thick card, using a saucer to make the shape.

3 Position small shells to form a pattern on the cardboard crescent and glue them in position using a glue gun.

4 Make the base for the urn from driftwood and shells, breaking them into evenly-sized pieces. Glue them in position on the lid of the tea box.

5 Position the crescent of shells over the urn base and glue in place.

6 Wind pieces of wire around a paintbrush to form handles for the urn. Glue them in place.

Something fishy: *découpage tray*

Découpage is one of the oldest and most decorative ways of changing the surface of walls, floors, furniture or screens. Here, an enchanting tray is created from a garden seed box and an old book of prints; images from old magazines would work just as well. The art is to choose one theme – fish, sea birds or shells – then paint the tray in an appropriate colour. The tray shown here is based on the fresh, vibrant colours of the Mediterranean and finished off with chunky rope handles. If the chosen theme were sea birds, the tray could have been painted in greys with a splash of red or yellow.

YOU WILL NEED:

- **Garden seed box**
- **Screwdriver**
- **Piece of hardboard**
- **Pencil**
- **Saw**
- **Sandpaper**
- **Drill**
- **Glue gun and sticks**
- **Tacks**
- **Hammer**
- **Emulsion paint, in aqua-blue, blue and brown**
- **Fish images and paper**
- **Paintbrushes**
- **Scissors**
- **Piece of wood**
- **Masking tape**
- **Matt varnish**
- **Rope**

1 To remove the base of the box, insert a screwdriver between the side and the base and lever off. Mark a new base on the hardboard.

2 Cut out the new hardboard base using the saw, and sand down the edges to make them smooth.

3 Drill two holes in each end of the tray for the string handles.

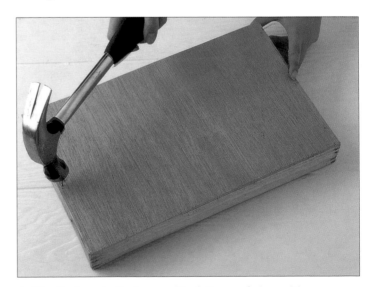

4 Glue the base to the tray and tack it securely in position.

5 Apply an even coat of aqua-blue emulsion paint to the tray, inside and out. Leave to dry thoroughly.

6 Paint the whole tray roughly with blue paint, making sure that the aqua-blue shows through in parts.

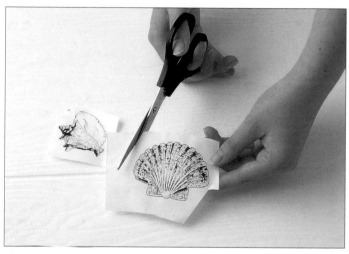

7 Cut out your shell and fish images. Enlarge the images on a photocopier if required.

8 Lay the images on a piece of wood and secure in place with masking tape.

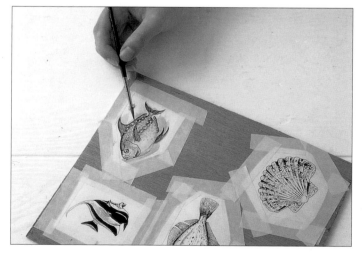

9 Brush a very watered-down wash of paint all over the images. Leave to dry thoroughly.

10 Remove the images from the wood and carefully cut them out. ➤

11 Position and glue the paper motifs on the tray as you like.
Varnish over the motifs on the tray, giving it at least three coats.

12 Cut two lengths of rope for the handles, and tape the ends with
masking tape. Push the rope through the holes.

13 Knot the ends of the rope securely to hold the handles in place.

Cast adrift: *driftwood boat*

Scour the beach for pieces of interestingly shaped driftwood and other flotsam and jestsam – it's a delightful and extremely therapeutic way to spend a day by the seaside. Sort through your finds and choose shapes that would instantly make a boat or a fish. You will be amazed at just how many uses there are for a humble piece of driftwood, given a little imagination and creativity. Fashion your discoveries into shapes, and within hours you could even have your own flotilla. If you are feeling a little more industrious, you could cut out the simple shape of a fish and mount this on to a stand made from a gloriously shaped beach find. Visually delightful when displayed on a windowsill or on a shelf in the kitchen or bathroom, you can keep them as a memento of a happy seaside holiday or give them as a lovely present to friends.

YOU WILL NEED:
- **Seaside finds**
- **Drill**
- **Craft knife**
- **Glue gun and sticks**
- **Flotsam, or fibre pot, for sail**

1 Decide on how you want your boat to look, then mark the position for the mast. Using a fairly small drill bit, make a hole in the driftwood.

2 Take the piece you will be using for the mast and file down the end to a slight point with a craft knife (remember to cut away from yourself to avoid accidents).

3 Squeeze glue into the drilled hole and fix the mast in place. Leave to dry thoroughly.

4 For the sail, fix the flotsam or torn-up fibre pot to the mast. If you like, use pieces of seaweed strung up to look like rigging.

Beach style: *sand gardens*

Create your very own container gardens using the most unusual of plantings. In place of pansies and daisies, grow small clumps of marram grass. Make pleasing patterns within the boxes with shells and coral. Broken tiles and stones alongside pieces of cork can be fashioned into a garden with an almost Japanese simplicity that would look at home anywhere, from a city apartment to a waterside cottage. Here, a selection of smaller boxes is used, but you could just as easily make up a larger one, support it on bricks, fill it, then cover the top with glass to make a delightful coffee table which is a focal point with its shoreline view.

YOU WILL NEED:
- **1 m x 1.5 cm (1 yd x ⅝ in) piece of wood**
- **Ruler**
- **Pencil**
- **Saw**
- **Wood glue**
- **Piece of hardboard or plywood, 25 cm (10 in) square**
- **Hammer**
- **Panel pins**
- **Sand**
- **Shells, broken china or seaside finds**

1 Cut the piece of wood into four pieces: two of 25 cm (10 in) and two of 23 cm (9 in) long, to form the square sides of the box for the sand garden.

2 Run a line of wood glue around the edge of the hardboard or plywood piece and position the wooden sides on this, with the same-size pieces facing each other. Leave to dry thoroughly.

3 Turn the box over and hammer in panel pins all the way around.

4 Fill the box with dry sand.

5 Work out your preferred design on the surface of the sand.

6 You could use pieces of broken china rather like mosaics and mix them with razor shells and sand dollars.

Seaside games: *bag of dominoes*

Hessian has a wonderful tactile quality, is extremely inexpensive and can be used for any manner of things. Here, it is used to great effect for a drawstring bag, filled with domino-painted pebbles. It's a fun idea that could be made either as a gift or while on holiday. The bag is quick to make and children would greatly enjoy finding and marking up stones as dominoes. Jute or hessian bags would also be perfect for holding marbles, dice or Chinese checkers.

YOU WILL NEED:
- **Hessian, 0.5 m (½ yd)**
- **Scissors**
- **Large-eyed tapestry needle**
- **Jute garden twine**
- **Pebbles**
- **Fine black marker pen**

1 Decide on what size you want your bag to be; it will have to be reasonably big because of the number of dominoes. Cut the hessian to twice the length required and fold the fabric in half. Pull some threads from the loosely-woven hessian to use for sewing up the bag.

2 Put the wrong sides together and, using the tapestry needle and hessian threads, slip stitch the opening down the sides and across the bottom. Then fray the sides by pulling out two to three strands to leave a fringed edging.

3 Draw down three threads 4–5 cm (1½–2 in) from the bag's top edge and again 2.5 cm (1 in) below this. Thread twine through the bottom line, picking up three strands at a time, to form the drawstring. Knot the ends so they won't fray.

4 Mark domino pips on the pebbles with a marker pen and place them in the bag. Don't make the pebbles too big or the bag will be very heavy.

Templates

The templates on these pages can be used at the same size or scaled up or down, using either a grid system or a photocopier. For the grid system, trace the template and draw a grid of evenly-spaced squares over your tracing. To scale up, draw a larger grid on to another piece of paper. Copy the outline on to the second grid by taking each square individually and drawing the relevant part of the outline in the larger square. Finally, draw over the lines to make sure they are continuous. To trace the templates, you will need a pencil, tracing paper and scissors.

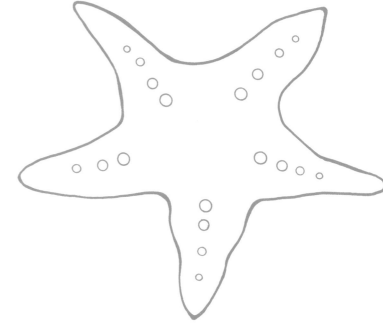

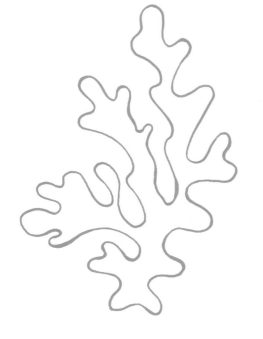

Shower curtain p 74–5

Glass carafe p 134–5

China p 136–8

Embroidered pillowcases p 69

Acknowledgements

Bazar
82 Golborne Road
London W10 5BS
Tel: 020 8969 6262
(Bedhead p 27, windbreak p 76,
squid vase p 157)

Bombay Duck
16 Malton Road
London W10 5UP
Tel: 020 8964 8882
(Glasses p 91)

Decorative Living
55 New Kings Road
London SW6 4SE
Tel: 020 7736 5623

Yves DeLorme
Tel: 01296 994 980

Dylon International Ltd
Consumer Advice Line: 020 8663 4296
(Dye for linens p 66-7)

The Finishing Touch & Design Ltd
Marsh Mills
Luck Lane
Huddersfield HD3 4AB
Tel: 01484 514463
(Bed linen on p 100-1)

Harley & Co. Antiques
295 Lillie Road
London SW6 7LL
Tel: 020 7381 5277
(Shell tables p 78, mirror and pot p 108)

The Kasbah
8 Southampton Street
London WC2E 7HA
Tel: 020 7240 3538
(Lanterns p 130)

Malabar
Unit 31-33, South Bank Business Centre
Ponton Road
London SW8 5BL
(Fabrics p 50)

The Mulberry Home Collection
41–42 New Bond Street
London W1Y 9HB
Tel enquiries: 01749 340594
(Cushions p 80, Director's chairs p 80-1)

The Nursery Window
83 Walton Street
London SW3 2HP
Tel: 020 7581 3358

Josephine Ryan Antiques
320 Lillie Road
London SW6 7PA
Tel: 020 7381 6003

PROJECT CONTRIBUTORS
Thanks to Helen Baird for the mosaic
table on p 111 and the mosaic bowl and
mirror on p 109; Emma Harding for the
rug on p 28 and the tray on p 146; Mandy
Pritty for the muslin seashore screen on
p 55; Jonty Henshall for the driftwood
beach chair on p79, the reclaimed timber
cupboard on p79, the kitchen cupboard on
p 82, the wooden wardrobe on p 82 and
the grandfather clock on p 83; Andrew
Ewing for the lamp base on p 111.

ACKNOWLEDGEMENTS
Many thanks to the Reeves family for their
hospitality and for the use of their home,
Judith Botten for her charming beach
house, Alison Davis for her assistance in
hand modelling, Sacha Cohen for her
paint techniques, Pat Grinsted for her
beautiful sewing of duffel bags and beach
house curtains and cushions, and Pat
Istead for her superb needlework on the
squab cushions. Special thanks to Charles
Shirvell without whose creativity, patience
and skill many of the projects would not
have been possible, to James Duncan for
the step photography. A huge thank you to
Spike Powell for his beautiful
photographs.

PICTURE ACKNOWLEDGEMENTS
The publishers would like to thank the
following for photographs used in this
book: Spectrum Colour Library: p 8 and
p 17 stones on the beach; p 2 and 12 beach
huts reflected in water; p 22 doorway,
Casares, Spain; Superstock: p 14 Ia,
Santorini, Greece; Riomaggiore, Italy;
p 18 Redondo Beach, California, USA;
p 19 Mykonos, Cyclades Islands, Greece;
p 29-30 harbour town of Yialos, Symi,
Greece; Marie Claire Maison: p 11 Nordic
summer cottage (photographer I. Snitt,
stylist D. Rozenztroch); Julian Nieman:
p 15 verandah, Anguilla, West Indies;
beach hut, Sri Lanka, © Julian Nieman;
Maggy Howarth: p 34 pebble fish mosaic.

Index